ESSENTIAL TENNIS

ESSENTIAL TENNIS

IMPROVE **FASTER**, PLAY **SMARTER**, AND **WIN** MORE MATCHES

Ian Westermann

with Joel Chasnoff

ST. MARTIN'S GRIFFIN   NEW YORK

Before embarking on the exercises suggested in this book, a reader should first consult with his or her physician who can make recommendations about the advisability of these suggested exercises based upon each reader's medical history and current medical condition.

First published in the United States by St. Martin's Griffin, an imprint of St. Martin's Publishing Group

ESSENTIAL TENNIS. Copyright © 2022 by Ian Westermann. All rights reserved. Printed in the United States of America. For information, address St. Martin's Publishing Group, 120 Broadway, New York, NY 10271.

www.stmartins.com

Designed by Richard Oriolo

Library of Congress Cataloging-in-Publication Data

Names: Westermann, Ian, author. | Chasnoff, Joel, author.
Title: Essential tennis : improve faster, play smarter, and win more matches / Ian Westermann ; with Joel Chasnoff.
Description: First. | New York : St. Martin's Griffin, 2022.
Identifiers: LCCN 2022000929 | ISBN 9781250765239 (trade paperback) | ISBN 9781250861108 (hardcover) | ISBN 9781250765246 (ebook)
Subjects: LCSH: Tennis. | Tennis—Training.
Classification: LCC GV995 .W47 2022 | DDC 796.342/2—dc23/eng/20220119
LC record available at https://lccn.loc.gov/2022000929

Our books may be purchased in bulk for promotional, educational, or business use. Please contact your local bookseller or the Macmillan Corporate and Premium Sales Department at 1-800-221-7945, extension 5442, or by email at MacmillanSpecialMarkets@macmillan.com.

First Edition: 2022

10 9 8 7 6 5 4

FOR MY STUDENTS

CONTENTS

Introduction   1

SECTION I: THE IMPROVEMENT PROCESS

1. Domination Delusion   15
2. You're Always Training Something   23
3. Feel Versus Real   29
4. Winneritis   37
5. Be Honest—How Good Am I?   46
6. Federer's Whiff and Serena's Volley   54
7. "Eureka!" Engineered   60

SECTION II: ON COURT

8. Effortless Power: The Kinetic Chain   71
9. There Is No Ball   79
10. Good Feels Bad   86
11. String Theory: Let Go of Control   92
12. Practice Mind, Match Mind   100
13. Lessons or Tournaments?   107
14. Do(n't) Copy the Pros   112
15. Trick and Treat   117
16. Pushers I: Shape   123
17. Pushers II: Over and In   131
18. Ultimate Tennis Warm-up   136
19. Against the Wind   146

20. Mini Tennis   152

21. Find Love at the Net   161

22. Play Like You Practice: The Great Swing-Speed   169
    Conundrum

23. Strategy: Plan A   178

24. Warm Up Like Sherlock Holmes   188

25. Eye off the Ball   197

26. (Not Necessarily) Better to Serve Than to Receive   205

27. Serves II: First and Second   210

28. Return-of-Serve I: Serve + 1   216

29. Return-of-Serve II: The X Factor   222

30. The Do-Nothing Volley   230

31. Lessons: The Student-Coach Partnership   236

32. Doubles Therapy I: Come Together   244

33. Doubles Therapy II: Meet My Lesser Half   251

SECTION III: THE MENTAL GAME

34. Mental Tennis Lies: Cry, Baby, Cry   261

35. Mental Tennis Truths: Emotional Shadow Swings   268

36. Dealing with McEnroes (and Lawn Mowers, and   276
    Babies, and Nadals)

37. Managing Tennis Energy: Intensity   283

38. Second-Set Slump   287

Conclusion: 291
"Finding Fulfillment: Love for the Tennis Journey"
    Transformation Stories

Appendix A: Glossary of Tennis Terms   303

Appendix B: 30 Progressions for Tennis Improvement   311

Appendix C: Match-Success Checklist   317

Acknowledgments   321

ESSENTIAL TENNIS

INTRODUCTION

What's the number one thing stopping you from playing your best tennis?

For many players, the answer is probably "Time"—that between work, family, and other obligations, there aren't enough hours to invest in training on court.

Others might say, "Age." If only they'd started taking lessons years ago, when their bodies were flexible and strong, and their minds fresh, they could have been the next Agassi/Serena/Roger.

Another legitimate concern is athletic ability. Like it or not, some of us are more naturally athletic than others. Our DNA and athletic history partly determine how far we go.

And, of course, there's what may be the biggest roadblock of all: "Money." Between rackets, shoes, strings, court time, and instruction, it can cost $50,000 to raise a top-level Junior player—*annually!* If you don't have fifty grand a year to put into tennis, you need to either find yourself a benefactor (like Simona Halep, whose training was financed by a Romanian businessperson), make sacrifices (like the Djokovic family), or be lucky enough to have a parent or friend who'll coach you for free (like Richard Williams, father of Serena and Venus, or Gloria Connors, mother of Jimmy). Tennis is one of the more accessible sports, but there's no question that money can help you reach your goals.

There are other obstacles to improvement. Difficulty finding practice partners and lack of access to quality coaching and facilities come to mind.

Yet, based on my thirty years in the game and more than twenty thousand hours coaching thousands of students, I can confidently say that there's an even bigger obstacle out there—an obstacle you probably never thought of, but that's holding you back from playing to your highest potential:

The ball.

You might think this sounds ridiculous. The whole point of tennis is to hit the ball over the net and inside the lines, so how can the ball be the thing that's standing in the way?

In fact, this is *why* the ball is such an impediment: Your desire to hit a good shot, with the right mix of power and spin and to a specific spot on the court, prevents you from striking the ball the way you should.

If only there were magical tennis balls that disappeared into thin air the instant they touched the racket strings! That way, you couldn't obsess over the flight of the ball, where it lands, or how fast it travels. Instead, you'd be free to focus on how you *feel* as you set up and swing to contact: "Am I balanced? Am I loose, or tense? Is there enough space between my body and the ball so that I can swing freely and strike the ball where I want to relative to my body, instead of the ball deciding for me?"

Alas, such magical tennis balls don't exist. Instead, you need to do the next best thing: Take the ball out of the equation entirely—to say to yourself, "There is no ball." This means practicing movement and swing technique without regard for what the ball does after you hit it. Because like it or not, your desire for a successful outcome—in this case, to "hit a good shot," with what you think is the right amount of power and spin, to a certain place on the court—will override your ability to move and swing correctly.

To make matters worse, your urge to create a certain result causes something else: bodily tension. Muscles become tight and your heartbeat quickens as you attempt to exert control. This is subconscious—a remnant of the caveman version of you who relied on fight-or-flight reactions to cope with imminent danger. Flexed muscles and a quickened heart rate are great if you're trying to flee a tiger. They're less helpful, however, for hitting a backhand.

But "no ball" isn't just a metaphor for training. The key to hitting a tennis ball with maximum power and spin is to swing the racket *as if there were no ball*. Instead, the ball just happens to be in the path of your racket strings, allowing you to remain loose and relaxed.

Over the course of these thirty-eight chapters and the supporting content online, you'll learn how getting better at tennis actually happens. I'll also teach you how to easily implement what you learn and integrate it into better play on court. You'll hit stronger shots, make fewer errors, and beat players who are currently beating you. The end result is that you will become a better player.

This book is every bit as much for coaches as for players. My hope is that the material in it inspires coaches to look differently at what it means to provide a student with a holistic learning experience.

Essential Tennis contains technique-based instruction on how to execute ground strokes, volleys, and serves—instruction that has proven successful over twenty years with clients of all ages and skill levels. The book is about the improvement journey itself, including the progressions, drills, and mindsets you should incorporate into your training in order to play to your highest potential.

Much of what you'll learn is counterintuitive, including:

- Why often the best thing to watch is *not* the ball.
- How you can hit your tennis shots with dramatically

increased power and spin by using less effort, not more.

- The shocking reality of how often professional players make the very same mistakes you do.
- Why correct technique often feels terribly wrong.
- A new perspective on victory, defeat, and what it means to be "dominant," through the example of one of my favorite players—Rafael Nadal.

And there's plenty more.

This book, like my teaching philosophy, is founded on two principles:

1. For every aspect of tennis, there is one element that's more important than any other.
2. If you can make even a tiny improvement in that element, you will become a better player much faster than if you focused on other things.

These two principles apply to every facet of the game—whether it's strokes, movement, strategy, or mental toughness and your attitude on court.

To be clear: There are probably a dozen things you could do right now to make, say, your forehand better. But what I'm saying is that there's *one* element that, if you improve it, will lead to the greatest impact in the shortest amount of time. I've dedicated the last thirty years of my life to pinpointing these essential elements so that my students can experience big improvements quickly.

A perfect example is a recent YouTube video I posted called *Aim Here for Easy Winners*. In the video, I explain how to win more points simply by noticing when your opponent is out of position—and then hitting into the open court.

Within days of posting the lesson, I received comments from players who'd gone out and played with that one simple focus in mind and had already experienced significant results:

> "These basic principles . . . have taken me from
> 5–6 games off a very strong player to winning 1–2
> sets every time we play, and I haven't changed my
> technique at all."

And:

> "I went to the court last night with this video in mind
> and decided to keep my strategy as simple as possible,
> following the principles you showed here. I usually
> beat my tennis mate, but this time the win came much
> easier—I almost didn't run at all . . . I caught myself
> smiling during the points noticing how many times my
> mate put himself in a running situation. All I had to do
> was punish his bad shot selection."

I'd like you to notice three things about these comments. First, these players didn't change a single thing about their technique. Players below the 5.0 level tend to believe that the only way to win more matches is by improving technique—but this example shows that technique is but one element in your arsenal.

Second, this example demonstrates that big improvements can happen fast. It didn't take months or years for these players to play better. Because the tip was simple to understand and easy to execute, they were able to experience improvement fast.

Finally, this lesson is proof that you can get better at tennis by consuming content on your own, without a coach standing next to you. It's always great to have a good coach by your side, but the reality is that good coaching is expensive and often hard to find. My teaching is founded on the idea that players can improve on their own, so long as the method is simple and sound. This book is a culmination of that philosophy. I'm confident that if you focus on these essential elements in the way I recommend, the game of tennis will become significantly easier for you and you will become a better player. This will include:

- Being able to hit the type of shot you want, when you want to hit it.
- Beating opponents you've always lost to.
- Thriving in competition instead of crumbling under pressure.
- Knowing how to fix mistakes in the moment and self-evaluate at every stage of the improvement process, on your own.

How to Use This Book

I wrote *Essential Tennis* for players at every level. If you're experienced with the game and familiar with the terminology, the layout of the court, and rating systems, I suggest you dive right into chapter 1. If, however, you're new to tennis, returning to the game after a hiatus, or the parent of a tennis-playing child without a deep knowledge of tennis yourself, I recommend you review the material at the back of the book first. You'll find a glossary of common tennis terminology, explanations of the various grips, and an introduction to the rating systems that players, coaches, and leagues use to categorize levels of play.

I also include a diagram of the tennis court. Even if you've been playing since you were a kid, you should review this map and refresh your memory. What you find might surprise you! For example, what's greater—the width of the doubles alley or the height of the net at the posts, and by how much? (Or are they equal?) If you're not sure, flip to the back and take a look. The answer has important implications for strategy.

As for the chapters themselves: I laid out the content in such a way that will provide the most benefit to the typical player when it's read in order. For this reason, I recommend that the first time you read the book, you read the chapters in sequence. Then, once you're familiar with the ideas and my teaching philosophy, feel free to dip in and out of the book as you choose, based on whatever help you happen to need at the moment. If you find yourself overwhelmed with nerves, flip to the chapter on Stan Wawrinka's pre-match breakdown.

Should you happen to be playing one of those matches where, for the life of you, you just can't seem to hit any of your shots in, pull out the book during the next changeover and browse the chapter on how to self-correct. I envisioned the book as something you might carry along in your tennis bag, along with wristbands and extra grips. Short of having me right there with you on the court, it's the next best thing.

Video: Because You Don't Know What You Don't Know

Regardless of what chapter you happen to be reading or where you are in your own personal tennis journey, I want to make clear that the advice in this book will help you only to the extent that you know how to self-assess. At any given moment, you need to be able to know how well you're executing the technique, movements, strategy, and mental attitude you're trying to improve. Self-assessment is one of the hardest parts of getting better at anything. But now, thanks to the video camera on your smartphone, you can measure your progress and know exactly how well (or not) you're playing.

In chapter 3, I talk about why filming yourself is critical if you want to improve. I also explain how and where to set up your camera. For now, I'll leave it at this: If you're not filming yourself, you're only guessing. You might think you know what needs to be fixed, and after a few reps, you might even be convinced that you've fixed it. But until you see the proof on a screen, you can never be sure. I realize it might feel like a pain to set up a tripod and phone every time you hit—but I assure you that once you do, the only complaint you'll have is that you didn't do it sooner. While there are no shortcuts to success, you can hack the process, shaving years and even decades of practice time, by assessing yourself with video.

Speaking of video: Twelve chapters in *Essential Tennis* have a corresponding web page online where you'll find video demonstrations, along with PDF downloads. Utilizing these tools will help you understand the concepts you read in the book more fully and, more important, will help you implement them much faster, especially if you happen to be more of a visual or auditory learner.

The easiest way to access this supporting content is to simply scan the QR codes at the end of relevant chapters. (QR code functionality is built into the camera app of all Apple and Android smartphones. No additional app or download is needed!) You can also visit EssentialTennis.com and see the content there.

Improvement: How Do You Know?

Since one of the main goals of *Essential Tennis* is to make you a better tennis player, it's worth asking what that actually means. More wins? Fewer errors? Moving up a level in your league—from, say, 3.5 to 4.0?

The answer is different for every player. But one way you might think of it is this: What would it take for you to beat the player you are now in three months, 6–0, 6–0? Which weaknesses would you need to shore up and which strengths would you have to maximize in order to "double-bagel" yourself? I'd encourage you to spend a few minutes pondering those questions and writing down a few notes, because the answers will effectively pave a path for you to follow.

On that note: To maximize your improvement, I suggest you start keeping a tennis journal. As they say in Silicon Valley: You can only manage what you can effectively measure. On the tennis court, this means keeping track of what happens during practices and your matches. It doesn't have to be complicated. Keep it simple, so you don't get overwhelmed or dread maintaining it. After every training session, simply jot down a few sentences about what went well and what could have been improved. Do it without judgment. Just make it an objective reflection on what worked out as you'd hoped and what adjustments you might make so that next time you'll play better.

Take a similar approach to match play, but add a few sentences about your opponent, like his or her style of play and strengths and weaknesses, and what you might do differently next time you square off. Also note how you managed the match overall. As I tell my students, every tennis match is a storybook, complete with a beginning, middle, and end. To be successful on court, you need to objectively observe what's happening in the story of that particular match, and then react with real-time adjustments. (In the online content for the book, I've included sample journal pages from some of my students.)

As your skill-building journey gets under way, I want to thank you for becoming a part of the Essential Tennis family. I published my first blog post from my basement apartment in Maryland in February 2008. Now, more than a decade later, my coaching videos have been viewed more than one hundred million times by eleven million players and coaches in more than one hundred fifty countries. What moves me most is the variety and range of people who participate— players in their eighties and nineties, competitive Juniors, young parents and empty nesters, college players, gold ball winners, NCAA coaches, and a number of players who have Association of Tennis Professionals (ATP) and Women's Tennis Association (WTA) points. Though their backgrounds differ, they are united by their passion for tennis—and for getting better, slowly but surely, at this wonderful game. I'm honored to be part of their lives. And I'm so happy to count you among them.

THE IMPROVEMENT PROCESS

1

Domination Delusion

Anytime I take on a new student, I ask him or her if they have a specific goal, something in particular they want to work on.

Most want to add power and spin to their ground strokes. A few want to improve their serve. Some even want to concentrate on their footwork.

And then there was one recent new student who caught me totally off guard with his request:

"I want to win every point," he declared.

I've been teaching tennis for twenty years. In that time, I've pretty much heard it all.

But, seriously?

Every single point?

"It's so frustrating!" he went on. "I win a point, then the other guy wins a point. Then I win a few, he wins a few, and back and forth . . ."

I told my new student, as gently as I could, that "I win a few, then he wins a few" is *exactly* how a tennis match is supposed to go. Not only at his level, but at every stage of competitive play, from red-ball kiddie tennis to the ATP Tour.

"Not only that," I continued, "but would you actually *want* to win every point? I mean, think about it—would you enjoy tennis if it were 6–0, 6–0, all games love in your favor, every time you played?"

I, for one, would not; I have a feeling you wouldn't either. (If you did, you'd only seek out opponents who are weaker than you.) And it made me realize that herein lies one of the biggest secrets of tennis success:

You have to enjoy the ride.

Yes, it sounds cliché. But when it comes to tennis, it's true: Ours is a back-and-forth sport, and if you don't enjoy the seesaw nature of the game, you might as well quit. It's one of the few sports where it's pretty much guaranteed you won't shut out your opponent. And unlike baseball, soccer, hockey, and other traditional sports, tennis is one of the few where your opponent gets a point every time *you* screw up.

So instead of resisting the idea that your opponent is going to score, embrace it. Enjoy the back-and-forth nature of the competition—the thrill of building a lead, losing it, and (ideally) taking it back.

In fact, when I think of the term "great competitor," what comes to mind is *not* a player who wins all or even most of his points, but someone who relishes the struggle and refuses to quit despite the struggle.

A perfect example is Rafael Nadal.

What makes Rafa the ideal case study for this chapter is that he's the ultimate competitor. He plays just as hard whether it's 6–6 in a tiebreak or he's up two sets to love. He's also one of the most dominant players of all time—especially on clay. Of the seventeen French Opens in which he's competed, Nadal has won the tournament thirteen times. That's 105 out of 109 matches—a winning percentage of 96 percent!

Nadal's French Open dominance would seem to contradict the whole "I win a few, then he wins a few" idea I mentioned earlier.

But does it?

Could it be that Rafa isn't quite as dominant as we think?

Before we dive into the stats behind Nadal's French Open wins, I want to introduce my friend and fellow tennis professional Craig O'Shannessy. Craig is an expert on strategy. He's also obsessed with statistics. You can read more about him on his website, BrainGameTennis.com.

In a May 2014 article for *The New York Times*, Craig examined Rafael Nadal's domination—or supposed domination—at the French Open. (Since the article, Nadal has won the French Open five more times.)

At the time of the article, Rafa had won eight of the nine French Open tournaments in which he competed. His match record during that span was an incredible 59–1, for a winning percentage just over 98 percent.

In those sixty French Open matches, Rafa played a total of 196 sets. Craig found that Nadal won 177 of those sets and lost only 19, a winning percentage of 90 percent—a bit lower than before, but still undeniably dominant.

Craig then dissected Nadal's 196 sets into games and found something surprising about Nadal's "dominance": Of the 1,804 games Nadal played, he won 1,169 and lost 635—a winning percentage of 65 percent.

Is a 65 percent winning percentage against the best tennis players in the world impressive? Absolutely. Is it dominant? Not like before.

But here's the part of Craig's study that really got me:

When Craig broke down Nadal's sixty French Open matches into individual points, he discovered that Rafa had won 6,465 points and lost 4,920, a winning percentage of—are you ready for this?—56 percent.

In other words: Rafael Nadal, the thirteen-time French Open champion and undisputed greatest clay-court player of all time, lost 44 percent of his points in his first nine appearances at the French.

I've summarized Craig's findings here:

RAFAEL NADAL AT THE FRENCH OPEN: 2005–2013

	Total Played	Won	Lost	Winning Percentage
Matches	60	59	1	98 percent
Sets	196	177	19	90 percent
Games	1,804	1,169	635	65 percent
Points	11,385	6,465	4,920	56 percent

Or think of it like this: Had Nadal lost instead of won just 7 percent more of the points played, he would have *zero* French Open titles.

You might be wondering (as I did) if this phenomenon is unique to Nadal at the French Open.

The answer is a resounding "No." In 2018, Roger Federer won about 54 percent of the points he played. So did Novak Djokovic. Every other player on the men's tour won even less.

In fact, another of Craig's studies found that the men's World No. 1 player, whoever it happens to be at the time, wins about 55 percent of his points.

And loses almost half.

What do these statistics mean for the rest of us?

As an educator and coach, I feel there are two big takeaways from Craig's findings—one soft, the other hard.

The "soft" takeaway is, not surprisingly, this: All of us—you, me, and anybody who plays the game—need to stop being so hard on ourselves. We tend to beat ourselves up over every error, curse ourselves when our opponent hits an ace. This not only feels bad, it negatively impacts our game by breaking our concentration and making it likely we'll lose even *more* points as the match goes on.

Instead, we would all do well to remind ourselves that if the World No. 1 is allowed to lose 45 percent of his points, so are we. On that note, here's my first prescription of the book: The next time you make an error or your opponent makes a great shot, tell yourself—out loud—that this is just one of the 45 percent he's *supposed to* get.

And then move on.

The second lesson—the one I call the "hard" takeaway—has to do with strategy. Too often, players change tactics based on losing a single point, when what they *should* do is stay the course and dismiss the point as an anomaly. For example, let's say you hit a forehand down-the-line and then follow it to the net for a put-away volley—a smart, high-percentage play that, statistically, will likely pay off. Except that somehow your opponent gets a racket on the ball and hits a beautiful lob right over your head for a winner.

That's the last time I come to the net! you think. *I can't let her burn me twice.* And you play the rest of the match from the baseline, all because of one isolated lob.

In a way, you're correct: By refusing to come to the net, you take away your opponent's ability to lob you again. But you've inadvertently done something else: abandoned your entire game plan—an intelligent game plan that was probably working fine. What's a better approach? Give your opponent a thumbs-up for her fantastic shot, then say to yourself, out loud like before, "I guess that's one of the points she's supposed to get."

The pros all know this, by the way. The next time your favorite player gets aced, watch how he reacts. Chances are he'll just shake his head and move over for the next serve. No drama, no outburst. Because he not only *knows* he's going to lose almost half the points, he *expects* it.

This doesn't mean the pros don't try their hardest to win every point they can; it means that when they don't, it's not the end of the world. They know it's just one of the 45 percent their opponent is allowed.

And what if you end up losing a match? I wouldn't get too down about that, either. Chances are you didn't get crushed; you probably just lost a few more points than your opponent. A double fault here, a couple balls long there—that's all it takes in tennis to separate win from loss.

And, hey—you never know: It's even possible you won the *majority* of overall points but still lost the match, because of tennis's unique winner-takes-all scoring system. According to Craig, this happens in one out of every twenty professional matches.

So why begin with this information? Why not start with how to hold a racket, or what to look for when hiring a coach?

It's because I want you to have the right perspective. As we embark on our journey of tennis improvement, you must never forget that what we're striving for here is excellence, not perfection. Even if you add twenty miles an hour to your serve, master the art of topspin, and steel yourself with the mental toughness of a lion, you're still going to lose almost half your points. That's the reality of tennis—and what makes the game so great.

Rafael Nadal knows this. The next time he wins a title, watch how he collapses on court after victory. Then think about *why* he falls to the ground and spreads his arms like a child in the snow, and maybe even cries. Is it because he had an easy ride through the tournament, breezing past one opponent after the next, point after point? Or is it because he fought tooth and nail against the best tennis players in the world, endured injury and fatigue, yet managed to scrape up just *barely* enough points to win the title—and because he doesn't take his victory for granted?

2

You're Always Training Something

Suppose you decide that enough is enough—it's time to fix your backhand.

You don't know exactly what's wrong with it. All you know is . . . well, it stinks.

So you make a plan: Weekdays after work, you'll stop at the park and hit backhands against the wall. Weekends, you'll play a match or hit with a friend. You commit to training thirty minutes a day, no matter what. When it rains, you'll do shadow swings in your garage.

After three weeks, you haven't missed a day. So you decide to take the plunge: As an early birthday gift to yourself, you buy a ball machine. Now, in addition to hitting against the wall, you hit off the machine after work and for an hour on weekend mornings. To stay motivated, you print out a photo of Djokovic hitting a backhand and hang it on your wall.

Do you get tired of all these backhands? Yes. But you know what they say: "Practice makes perfect." Like a baby learning how to walk, you're going to stick with it until your body figures it out.

Six months later, your hard work and dedication have paid off—you're *awesome*. Here is, specifically, what you're awesome at:

Preparing late. Top-level tennis players turn their upper body extremely early, the instant they recognize that the incoming ball is headed to their backhand side. You, meanwhile, turn your body at the last possible moment. Late preparation leads to late contact—one of the reasons your backhand often goes into the net. You used to be good at preparing late, but now, after all this training, you're great at it.

Chopping at the ball instead of swinging up and through. An up-and-through swing path leads to net clearance, depth, and spin. You, meanwhile, have perfected the art of swinging flat, then collapsing your arms, with almost no follow-through—a recipe for unforced errors.

Keeping your weight back. One of the reasons you decided to fix your backhand was because it lacked power.

The reason? Instead of transferring your weight forward into the shot, you kept your body weight back. Thanks to all this rigorous practice, you're now awesome at it— you keep your weight back on every single backhand you hit.

It's true: Practice makes perfect!

You are always training something.

Every time you step onto the court, you either reinforce existing habits or consciously create new and better ones.

That's it. It's either one or the other: You're either getting "better" at what you already do, or you're learning the new behaviors that will take you to the next level of play. There is no in-between.

It's time to evolve past the notion that if you hit enough balls off the machine, you'll magically become a better player, that by repeating a certain action over and over, your body will "figure it out."

Unfortunately, phrases like "Practice makes perfect," "Gotta get in my reps," and "Just putting in my ten thousand hours" reinforce the idea that if you do something enough times, you'll get better at it. What these expressions miss is the role of *habit*—and the ironclad grip habits have on how we behave.

A habit is any behavior you perform automatically, without thinking. How you brush your teeth, how you hold a pencil, and how you hit a backhand are all habits. You've performed these actions so many times the same way that the neural pathways associated with them are hardwired in your brain.

Dr. Wendy Wood, a psychology professor at USC and author of *Good Habits, Bad Habits*, found that more than 40 percent of our daily actions are done habitually. From an evolutionary perspective, this is good: The more we can do without thinking, the more brainpower is left for actions that are essential to our survival, like gathering food, pursuing a mate, and choosing between two similarly priced tennis rackets.

Forty percent might sound like a pretty high number. On a tennis court, it's even higher. Here's how I phrase it to my students:

> When you play tennis, you are 100 percent the sum of your habits minus whatever conscious effort you dedicate to moving away from them.

Returning to our earlier example: Your backhand was poor because you had poor habits. And because you didn't consciously change any of your habits, all your diligent practice did was ingrain your bad habits more deeply into your brain.

To frame it in terms of the pros: One reason that Serena Williams's forehand is better than yours, mine, and pretty much everyone else's on the planet is not because she's hit tens of thousands more forehands than we have, but because she hit them correctly. She was also extremely conscious of how she was hitting them at first, until finally it became a habit. At this point, the movements are so ingrained that she doesn't have to think about it.

The key phrase in the above paragraph is "conscious of how she was hitting them." Tennis isn't like learning to walk—our bodies won't just "figure it out." This is why simply hitting a million balls against the wall or off a machine isn't enough.

To be clear: If you're happy with how you play now, and you want to continue beating the players you already beat and losing to the ones who already beat you, then by all means, buy a ball machine or go hit at the wall. You'll get more consistent and precise at what you already do.

But if you want to take your game to the next level, ten thousand hours of mindless practice won't cut it. It will push the next level farther from your reach, because your current habits will become more permanently ingrained.

This might sound daunting—the fact that every time you pick up a racket you're either getting better or more deeply ingraining bad habits.

But I like to think of it as an opportunity. For starters, it means you can get better anytime, anywhere. Want to improve your serve, which you currently hit with a forehand grip? Simply pick up your racket a few times throughout the day and hold it in a Continental grip for ten minutes. When you watch a match on TV, improve your footwork by doing a split-step every time the player at the top of the screen hits the ball. It doesn't matter if you're standing or sitting—pairing "other guy hits ball" with the action of a split-step starts to build muscle memory that you carry with you onto the court.

Second, and more important: Now that you know how improvement happens, you can speed up the process by practicing correctly. Instead of wasting time mindlessly hitting balls and thinking your body will somehow "get it," you can do purposeful, focused progressions that simultaneously build new and better habits while pushing old ones aside.

Next time you head to the courts and your spouse or partner asks where you're going, tell the truth: "I'm heading out to rewire the synaptic connections between backhand-related neurons in my cerebral cortex."

If they have no idea what you're talking about, explain, "I'm playing in a big tournament next month. Two hundred people from all over the state are coming to find out who has the best habits."

REFLECT

Think about one stroke you've tried to improve in the past that still needs work. Now that you're aware of the role of habits, how might you go about fixing that stroke today?

3

Feel Versus Real

If you have twenty-five dollars to spend on tennis and not a penny more, here's what I suggest you do:

1. Read this chapter.
2. Return this book to wherever you bought it and get your money back.
3. Spend the money on a tripod for your phone.

My publisher probably won't be thrilled I just said that. But I'm adamant. If you want to get better at tennis, it's essential that you film yourself when you practice and play, and then watch the footage afterward. Video is the only way to know that you're doing what you want to be doing.

You could also think of it in the reverse: If you don't use video, you're merely guessing.

That's right—*guessing*. We humans are good at many things, but one thing we're not good at is knowing what our bodies are doing at any given moment. The technical term for this mind-body perception gap is *biomechanical dissonance*. I prefer to call it "feel versus real."

"Feel versus real" means that your body *feels* like it's doing one thing while in reality it's doing something else. The consequence is that most players, including you, have no idea what they're actually doing on the tennis court. You think you do, but you don't. Don't believe me? You can experience feel versus real for yourself with this quick experiment. Read the instructions first, since you need to do it with your eyes closed:

Stand with your legs shoulder-width apart.

Spread your arms wide, as far as they'll go.

Close your eyes.

Keeping your arms straight, slowly bring your hands toward each other, like a slow-motion clap, until your fingertips are as close as they can possibly be *without touching*. Then, when you think your hands are as close as possible without touching, open your eyes to see the result.

Try it.

What happened?

If you're like most people, your fingertips either touched or your hands remained a lot farther apart than you expected. Without being able to watch your hands move, you lose track of where they are in space. You end up feeling like they're farther apart or closer than they are.

Here's how feel versus real plays out on the tennis court:

- Players insist they're bending their knees, but then they watch the film and see that their legs are almost perfectly straight.
- Players think they're swinging low-to-high. On film, it's clear their swing is flat.
- Players think their nondominant arm is straight throughout the serve toss. When they see the film, they realize their arm is bent at the wrist and elbow.

Feel versus real isn't restricted to movement and technique. Players think they're hitting crosscourt, only to see on film that they hit most shots down-the-line (a far riskier play). They'll insist they got burned down the alley a dozen times by an opponent, when in reality it only happened twice. They have no concept of where their shots land on the court—they'll tell me that most of their shots land deep, in no-man's-land, then we'll look at film and see that the majority bounce inside the service line.

What's important in all of these examples is that when I ask students what happened, they don't say, "I have no idea." They have a clear idea. But their idea is wrong. They're completely out of touch with reality.

The sad consequence is that players will spend months, years, or even entire careers trying to fix what they think is the problem when the problem is actually something else. Or, they believe they're fixing the problem when all they're doing is the same thing as before.

Video is the cure for all of this. The camera doesn't lie; it will put you in touch with reality immediately and objectively. In addition to closing the feel-real gap, video allows you to:

1. **Diagnose.** It's not enough to know that your forehand stinks. Video tells you exactly what the problem is, objectively. Without video, you're guessing.

2. **Prescribe.** Once you identify the problem, you can choose an appropriate solution. This way, you won't waste time pursuing the wrong cure.

3. **Verify.** Not using video is like doing math without checking the answers. With video, you can verify that you're executing technique correctly.

4. **Remember.** How many times have you taken a tennis lesson only to think, *That was great! What did we do?* Film your lessons for a record of what you learned, the progressions you did, and reminders of what to work on for next time.

5. **Understand.** "How did I lose to that guy?" we've all

asked at some point. When you film your matches, you can see objectively why you won or lost. Spoiler alert: It's most likely not what you think. Players often blame losses on faulty technique, when in reality it's poor shot selection or bad tactics.

6. **See proof . . .** that you're getting better. Improvement is sometimes a slow go—so slow that you might wonder if you're getting better at all. There's nothing better than watching old footage of yourself, seeing how bad you were, and then realizing how far you've come.

Despite the benefits of video (and the consequences of not utilizing it), most tennis players still don't use it. Often, they're simply embarrassed. They feel weird setting up a tripod on court, and they're afraid of what their opponent or hitting partner might say. My response is: "Get over it!" It's your life, your improvement journey, so who cares what they think?

But if you're still not comfortable, explain to your partner that you're working on your game, so you're filming yourself. Then offer to share the video so they can analyze their own game. More often than not, they'll take you up on the offer—they've probably never seen themselves play and will be intrigued by the idea.

The first time you see yourself on film, you'll probably be shocked. It's like that icky feeling of hearing your voice on tape, except worse, because you've spent so much time and effort trying to get better, only to discover you don't look nearly as good as you'd hoped. As one of my students put it: "I imagined I look like Federer. Then I saw myself on film, and I'm not even close."

But similar to how your voice on tape sounds strange to you but normal to everyone else, how you look playing tennis is weird only to you. To everyone else, it's how you always look playing tennis. Anyway, better to face the truth now, even if it's ugly, than to waste time thinking you're better than you are, or that you're improving when you're actually not.

TAKE ACTION

In the online content for this chapter, I demonstrate how to set up the camera depending on what you're working on.

Here's a summary:

Camera position for technique analysis: either directly to the side of contact (ground strokes and volleys) or directly behind contact (serves and overheads). Place the camera close enough so that you fill most of the screen, from your feet all the way up to the top of your racket's path.

Camera position for point play and strategy analysis: directly behind the middle of the baseline, as far back and as high up as you can get it (think TV broadcast camera angle). The goal is to look right down the center of the court.

Best camera and app for technique analysis: your smartphone! Most new phones now have a "slow motion" setting. Or, use an inexpensive app like OnForm (the one I use with my students) for extra features like drawing lines, angles, and side-by-side comparisons.

Best camera for point play and strategy: Your smartphone will work fine, but battery and storage can become an issue. When shooting with your phone for point play, simply use the "video" setting on your camera app; don't switch over to "slow motion." For better battery, more storage, and a wider field of view, check out any generation of tiny GoPro cameras.

Once you've got your camera set up, you can start with some progressions:

Progression 1

Film yourself playing, watch the film afterward . . . and that's it. Any angle, any camera, tripod or not. In this initial progression, the aim is to get over the biggest hurdle—filming yourself for the first time.

Progression 2

Film yourself a second time. When watching the footage, look for an example of feel versus real—find one thing you thought you were doing that seeing yourself on film helped you realize you weren't.

4

Winneritis

A few years ago, I asked one of my prospective clients to do a thought exercise. Dan, as we'll call him, was thinking about working with me, but he wasn't sure it'd be "worth it" because of how busy his lifestyle is. He works in advertising and travels at least once a month. When he's home, he's either working ten-hour days or spending time with his wife and three children. So, although he dreamed of improving from a 3.5 tennis player to a 5.0, he didn't believe it was possible—not only because he wouldn't have the time but because of the sheer enormity of the leap. "I would have to become a whole different player," Dan said. "We're talking an entirely different universe."

I was intrigued by how he'd phrased it—"an entirely different universe." It gave me an idea. I asked Dan to close his eyes and "see" himself playing as a 5.0. Try it yourself: Close your eyes and envision yourself playing tennis at your optimum level. As you watch yourself play, pay close attention to the following:

What does your forehand look like? Your backhand?
How fast are your shots, and where do they land?

How do the points end?

What's the biggest difference between how you play now and your ideal level of play?

Close your eyes and take a few minutes to truly "see" yourself at your peak level.

So—how was it? What did you see?
Here's what Dan saw:

I crush the ball. My forehand is a missile—my opponent can't even get a racket on it. Same with my backhand. My shots land a few inches from the baseline, then skid past him while he stands there frozen in his tracks.

I put the ball exactly where I want it. When the other guy charges the net, I rip a backhand down-the-line for a winner. My shots are beautiful. I hit winners from incredible angles, from deep in my forehand corner to the opposite service box.

Just about every point ends with a winner. Since my opponent's really good too, we're exchanging rockets until one of us unleashes a shot that the other one can't return.

That's the biggest difference: I hit with tons of power, my shots go where I want them to, and I stop making stupid mistakes.

How about you? When you did the exercise, did you see something similar to what Dan saw? Something different?

Let's talk about the point of the experiment.

Dan thought it was a visualization exercise. "To play at 5.0, I need to believe I can do it. If I can see it in my mind, I can manifest it on the court."

I told Dan that his answer was beautiful. And totally wrong.

This exercise has nothing to do with self-actualization, self-limiting beliefs, or your potential for greatness. Quite the opposite: I used it to show Dan that he, like most players, is completely out of touch with how tennis points are won and lost, and with what it means to be a high-level player.

Before I explain, consider these stats from Wimbledon 2019:

	NUMBER	PERCENTAGE
TOTAL POINTS PLAYED	22,767	100 percent
POINTS THAT ENDED WITH A WINNER	7,191	31 percent
POINTS THAT ENDED WITH AN ERROR	15,576	69 percent
TOTAL FORCED ERRORS	8,656	38 percent
TOTAL UNFORCED ERRORS	6,920	31 percent

As you look at the numbers, notice three things:

1. More than twice as many points ended with an error than with a winner.
2. The percentage of winners was equal to that of unforced errors. These were errors that happened for no reason at all—the player was in balance and missed a completely routine shot.
3. These statistics were for the most elite players in the world, on grass—the fastest surface and the easiest to hit winners on.

Most recreational players are like Dan—they think "high-level tennis" means hitting winners. But even at the most elite level of tennis, most points end in errors. If you take away just one idea from this book, it's this:

Tennis is a game of mistakes—and your job as a tennis player is to do things that cause your opponent to make mistakes.

This is most likely different from how you've always thought about tennis. Most players assume that winning at tennis comes as a result of hitting amazing shots. In reality, it's more often a result of making your opponent play badly.

Don't get me wrong—incredible highlight-reel shots do happen. These shots are on the highlight reel for a reason—they're rare. More than two-thirds of the time, the point is going to end because one of the players screws up.

The ramifications of this idea are enormous—it changes your entire perspective on the game. For starters, strategy. I talk about strategy in chapters 23 and 24, but your basic strategy should always be this: Pick out your opponent's weakness and pound away at it over and over using high-percentage patterns. This means, by the way, that *your strategy changes from opponent to opponent, depending on what they're weak at!*

Second, it diminishes the value you put on winners. One easy way to distinguish low-level from high-level players is by paying attention to when and from where they attempt to hit winners. Low-level players are addicted to winners and will try to hit one anytime from anywhere—a phenomenon I call "winneritis." High-level players, meanwhile, wait until they have a genuine opportunity to attack.

Lastly, it changes our perspective on improvement. Dan (like most club-level players) believed "getting better" meant hitting harder, at more extreme angles and closer to the lines. So they either practice this or they never bother trying to improve at all because the task sounds too daunting.

But once you understand that tennis is a game of mistakes, you discover what "improvement" really means: developing tools that will cause your opponents to make errors and decrease your chances of making a mistake. Tools like:

- Shot tolerance under pressure—being able to keep a rally going and get the ball back over the net one more time.
- Hitting with depth.
- Hitting with net clearance.
- Hitting to safe targets, at least four feet from the lines.
- Developing shots that induce errors from your opponent.
- Tactics, strategy, and tennis IQ—including hitting crosscourt until you have a good reason not to (because the court is longer and the net lower), and knowing when to go for a winner and when to simply keep the point going.

Even though you'll never hear a TV commentator talk about net clearance on a highlight reel, these tools are more effective than winners and truer to how most points are won.

Best of all, these tools are easier to develop. Dan is a perfect example. Since he lives in Los Angeles and couldn't work with me in Milwaukee, I coached him remotely, focusing first on his backhand slice. The slice is as far from a flashy shot as you can get, but it's one of the best ways to stay in a point and induce an error. The combination of backspin and the low bounce puts opponents off balance and causes them to over-hit. Our arrangement was simple: Dan would film himself hitting his slice and send me the video. I'd then put together a practice plan consisting of the specific progressions he needed to do. Then he'd film himself doing the progressions, and back and forth we'd go, until, four months later, his slice was dramatically better than it had been.

Dan was suddenly able to beat players he hadn't before—not because he hit successive winners, but because he'd found a way to make his opponents screw up. As a bonus, his confidence increased—with a slice in his arsenal, he didn't feel he had to crush his opponents with highlight-reel winners that, frankly, he was incapable of hitting reliably. No longer feeling like he had to be Superman, he loosened up, felt less tense, and hit his other strokes with more accuracy and consistency.

Just so there's no misunderstanding—offense has its place in the game of tennis. Especially at higher levels of the game, you can't merely hit the ball back and wait for your opponent to make mistakes. You need to put your opponents off balance and *induce* mistakes, by hitting with power and spin to specific targets. Later on, in chapter 16, I'll teach you how to play with reliable offense, in which you hit with both power and consistency, so that you can dominate your opponents without shooting yourself in the foot.

For now, I want you to understand that reliable, consistent play should come first. When you see Federer and Serena hit powerful, awe-inspiring shots, allow their incredible play to inspire you—but don't make it the focus of your training on court.

TAKE ACTION

Progression 1

Go to your neighborhood courts or a nearby tournament, as a spectator. Notice when and from where on the court players attempt to hit winners. Then watch a college or pro match on video, and do the same thing. Do you see a difference between when and from where on the court the two levels of players try to hit winners?

Progression 2

Play a match, or hit competitively with a partner. Make a promise that you are not going to try for a winner unless you have a clear and undeniable opportunity to hit one. Keep the rally going until you get your chance. Pay attention to two things: how often your opponent will mess up without your having to do anything and how much easier it is to hit a winner when you wait for the right opportunity.

Progression 3

Think of a shot or skill you don't currently have that would help you induce errors from opponents; options might include a slice, drop shot, or kick serve. Then put together a plan for how to develop this skill. Use Appendix B to help guide you through the progressions correctly.

5

Be Honest—
How Good Am I?

Tennis players love to keep track of how good they are.
Whether it's their win-loss record, NTRP (National Tennis
Rating Program) to invented decimals ("I'm a 3.55 on hard
courts, 3.74 on clay"), or simply how they compare to others
("Better than Jane, same as Jill, not as good as Sue"), they have
various ways of knowing where they stand.

If, however, your goal is to get better at tennis, these
standard assessment measures will not do. Once you commit to getting better, these measurements become unreliable and might seem discouraging; because as you incorporate

new techniques, you're likely to lose more than you used to, until the new and improved movement patterns become habit.

What you need is an objective way of measuring your progress. The method I prefer is the Improvement Circle.

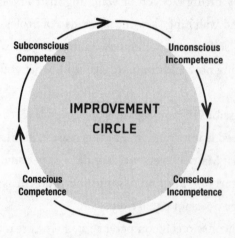

What's great about the Improvement Circle is that it explains how improvement actually happens and how far along you are in the process. It evolves from the most fundamental skill, such as how to hold your racket when hitting a serve. Then rises to the broadest manifestation of that skill—in this case, the ability to hit a powerful serve with tons of pace—in which hundreds of smaller skills are stacked.

Level 1: Unconscious Incompetence—
"I don't know what I don't know."

This is absolute zero: You're just beginning to learn a skill. At this stage, you're not aware of how to do it correctly—hence the term "Unconscious Incompetence."

When you're here, what you need most is *knowledge*. You get this by hiring a coach or watching instructional content online, and watching slow-motion video of professional players. You also film yourself in slow motion so you can see what you're doing now and compare that with what you should do instead.

Unconscious Incompetence is the easiest level to conquer—all you need is information. For this reason, it's also the most dangerous: Many players watch videos or get advice on how to hit a certain shot and assume the problem is fixed. But knowledge does not equal execution!

The Unconscious Incompetence stage is a great time to begin an Improvement Journal. In it, you'll state your goals, note what you learn, keep tabs of what progressions and drills you perform, and compare where you are now with where you want to be.

Level 2: Conscious Incompetence—
"I know what I'm supposed to do, but I can't do it yet."

In this stage, you teach your body to perform the movements you learned in Level 1.

You begin with slow, methodical repetitions of the proper movement. Your goal is to physically understand and feel the difference between your old habit and the one you're trying to learn. I start my students with segmented shadow swings, in which they pause at key checkpoints. Pausing allows them to be aware that they're hitting the positions they're supposed to. It also allows them to make multiple connection points— visual (they observe how they move), auditory (they hear my instructions), and kinesthetic (they feel the movement).

Slow-motion shadow swings typically come next, followed by "fake tosses," in which I toss a ball but the student doesn't try to hit it—the ball is for timing purposes only.

At the Conscious Incompetence stage, all work happens in a controlled environment. This means no rallies or point play. Trying to rally at this stage of improvement typically causes immediate reversion to old habits. It's a nonconscious force: When you focus on results, your most ingrained habits will take over.

In Appendix B, I list thirty progressions for mastering any particular skill. You'll find a print-ready version in the online content for this chapter, along with demonstrations of shadow swings and fake tosses.

This stage of the Improvement Circle is the one that's most often skipped. Players and coaches jump straight to rallying, without first ingraining the new movements into muscle memory. Players and coaches celebrate the first sign of competence. A player hits a great topspin forehand for the first time, coach and player high-five, and they move on to a different skill. It's important to realize that this rep is the first of many thousands needed before you can do it correctly without thinking.

As you work your way through Level 2, how do you know when you're ready to move on to the next progression? I look for 75 percent quality repetitions at a specific level of challenge before progressing to the next.

I want to reiterate that whether you're working with a coach or on your own, you *must* continue to film yourself and compare how you move now with how you want to.

Level 3: Conscious Competence—
"I can do it, but I have to think about it."

At this stage, you ingrain proper movements into habit. You do this through repetitions—thousands of them, each one performed consciously. It's the only way to wire a desired movement into a habit.

It's during Level 3 that hitting a ball is first introduced—but gradually. Begin with soft tosses from a coach, self-feeds, or hitting off a wall one shot at a time. Your goal is to execute the proper movement over and over, no matter what happens to the ball. Go slowly; if the level of challenge becomes too much, you'll revert back to old habits. For ground strokes, my students and I typically begin at the service line, then back up to no-man's-land, then to the baseline. Eventually, we do racket feeds that require movement, to simulate a real point. Then, and only then, will we move on to a cooperative rally.

Each step of the way, we pay attention to what conditions trigger a student's old habits. When this happens, we decrease the level of challenge until the student can execute comfortably at that level.

Throughout these repetitions, I have students reinforce their newly learned movements with shadow swings. I keep a video camera running, and we watch replays to heighten students' awareness of what they're actually doing.

As you get closer and closer to using your new habit in a "real life" environment, start paying attention to what happens to the ball. Do you make contact in the center of the racket? Where does the ball land? As my friend and fellow coach David Parker says, "The ball doesn't lie." The path of the ball always reflects what your racket was doing at contact. This is why you pay attention to results: not because you're obsessed with "success," but because what the ball does communicates how well you're executing the new movement.

It's important to note that once a ball is introduced, most players will regress to old habits. Level 3 is filled with steps forward and back, as new habits are ingrained against the influence of old.

Level 4: Subconscious Competence:
"I can do it without having to think about it."

This is the highest level of the Improvement Circle. Your goal now is to execute the new movement under pressure. To get there, many stepping-stones are required: Players should work their way up from feeds to cooperative rallies; then to cooperative challenge rallies in which there are targets or goals or only certain portions of the court are used; then to competitive rallies on either full or a portion of the court; and then to full-court sparring, where you don't keep score or you do (the most challenging step of all).

At this stage, your win-loss record is finally an appropriate way to measure whether you're improving. Even more important is whether you're beating players who used to beat you.

When you reach the end of the Improvement Circle, does progress suddenly stop?

Only if you're satisfied with your new level of play. Now that your technique is better, you'll beat players you couldn't beat before . . . and lose to players who used to be much better than you but who now are only a little bit better. To continue advancing, you'll need to improve all over again. The difference is that you're now starting at a higher baseline level.

That's why it's a circle: The improvement journey never ends. One challenge is accomplished, and another arises, providing another opportunity for growth.

TAKE ACTION

1. **Start an improvement journal.** Track your journey through the Improvement Circle, including what skills and progressions you do, what you learn, where you're coming along, and where you still need to improve.

2. **Map a skill.** Choose a tennis-related skill that you've always wanted to have but are currently missing. Map out how you might acquire this skill

on your own, using the four stages of the Improvement Circle as a guide:

Stage 1: Learn what good execution of the skill looks like.

Stage 2: Use segmented and slow-motion shadow swings to get a sense of what the correct movement feels like. Film yourself and then watch the video to make sure you're executing correctly.

Stage 3: Add a ball and slowly increase the level of challenge as you turn skill into habit. Rotate between shadow swings, self-feeds, and cooperative rallies with a partner or ball machine. Use video to verify correct execution.

Stage 4: Compete with your new skill in mind. If it flounders, interject a stepping-stone—an intermediary progression, so you can train yourself in a productive way and not be overwhelmed.

6

Federer's Whiff and Serena's Volley

I've watched thousands of hours of professional tennis in my life, both in person and on screen. During that time, I've seen our favorite players make egregious mistakes. Here are my all-time favorite three:

#1: Serena's Volley

I saw this live at the US Open. Serena Williams and sister Venus were playing doubles; Serena was at the net. The other team hit a weak floater to Serena's left. She poached toward the middle for the easy volley winner and hit a line drive directly into the stands.

#2: Federer's Whiff

This one I saw on TV. In the 2017 Laver Cup, Federer and Nadal teamed up as a doubles dream team. Federer, up at the net, received a low overhead that he and everyone else in the stadium expected he'd smash for a winner. He took two steps back, jumped, swung aggressively . . . and missed the ball completely.

#3: Querrey's Serve

I watched this one live at a different US Open. American Sam Querrey, at one point No. 11 in the world, prepared to serve. He bounced the ball a few times, coiled, tossed . . . and hit a rocket of a serve that landed two feet behind the opposing baseline—more than twenty feet out.

I love it when pros make ugly mistakes. Not because I want them to mess up, but because it reminds us that they're human beings, subject to the same laws of tennis physics as the rest of us. They make mistakes at higher speed and with more athleticism, but they struggle to get their bodies into perfect position and line up all the variables, same as we do.

Pro mistakes remind us of something else: Even when you have "perfect" technique, you're going to screw up. One of the biggest misconceptions recreational tennis players have is not realizing that they're going to, supposed to, and always will make mistakes. This in turn leads to another mistake: seeking out tips and tricks, in place of focusing on fundamentals. Any mistake you or any other tennis player on earth makes is because of a breakdown in essential technique, not because there's some secret trick that, if only you knew it, would make your mistakes go away.

This same idea applies to all the amazing shots our favorite players hit. We want to believe that Roger makes his down-the-line passing shot on the run because he possesses special talent or a trick reserved only for the tennis-enlightened. In reality, all great shots are the result of dozens of fundamental movements, all coordinated with incredible precision, in harmony at the same time.

Here are some of the more popular "tips" out there and why they're misguided. What's particularly dangerous is that many of these quick-fix cures have been around so long that they're accepted as law. You may have heard them yourself:

- **"Step into the ball."** If you have time to step in, you should. But often you won't, or you won't be in the right position to step in. Watch a pro match and notice that they step in a small percentage of the time.

- **"Carve around the ball for slice."** If you were to carve around the ball, you'd have no chance of hitting your serve in because the strings would be facing to the side at contact. You create slice by moving the racket past the ball from left to right (for a righty)—completely different from "carving around" it.

- **"Follow through over your shoulder."** Sometimes you will, sometimes you won't, but regardless, the follow-through shouldn't be engineered. It should be the result of movements you performed earlier in the stroke.

- **"Make contact in front of you."** Ideally, yes. But like the follow-through, it happens because you organized yourself before contact such that you could correctly execute the kinetic chain. You can't work on contact point on its own.

I understand why these quick fixes are so appealing. We live in a world of shortcuts and hacks, where the solution to every problem is always one click away. Plus, we *want* them to be true: How great would it be if you could add twenty miles an hour to your serve, if only you knew one little secret?

I promise you: When it comes to tennis, there are no shortcuts. Instead, focus on the four foundational principles that will work in every situation:

1. **Kinetic chain.** Using your big muscles in the correct order, from the ground up, leads to proper contact point, follow-through, and power.
2. **Angle of the racket face.** Wherever the strings are facing at contact, that's where the ball goes. Always.
3. **Swing path.** The degree to which you do or don't swing past the ball, versus through it, determines how much spin versus drive you have on your shots. When your racket travels straight through the ball

directly at your intended target, your shot won't have any spin; when the racket travels past the ball and away from your target, the ball spins as it travels toward the target.

4. **Efficiency vs. tension.** Tense muscles stop the body from moving in a fluid, relaxed way. The result is short strokes and choked-off power. Anxiety and a desire to exert control are two reasons players tighten up. Positioning too close to the ball is another.

It's tempting to think that when Federer, Serena, and other pros make mistakes it's because of some sophisticated reason beyond our scope and understanding. I assure you that their mistakes happen for the same reason yours do: a breakdown in one of the above four fundamentals.

TAKE ACTION

Progression 1

Watch a set of professional tennis. On a sheet of paper, keep track of how many errors each player makes. Take particular note of how many errors they weren't pressured into—they were in balance, weren't stretched out, and should have made the shot. Watching a player's errors accumulate, in ink on paper, drives home how common mistakes are, even for players who've perfected their technique.

Progression 2

Next time you hit or play a match, and you make mistakes, reflect on which of the four fundamentals broke down. If you're unsure which it was, refer back to the video you shot (hint, hint, nudge, nudge).

7

"Eureka!" Engineered

I love when students make breakthroughs. It's a thrill to see them work at a certain skill, persevere, struggle . . . and then, *Eureka!* They get it.

When I first started coaching, student breakthroughs were rare. When they did happen, it seemed to be by magic. These days, students experience breakthroughs every time I teach. Not because I'm a tennis wizard, but because after twenty years of coaching, I've discovered that there are things you can do to make breakthroughs more likely to happen.

I'm talking about *learning style*. Each of us learns differently; and how information is conveyed is as important as the information itself.

Breakthroughs happen when the right information is presented to the right student in the right way.

I discovered this in a eureka moment of my own. I was working my first paid coaching job at a club in D.C. One of my students was a fifty-year-old woman whom we'll call Denise. Over the course of six months, one lesson per week, we'd taken her game to a new level. . . .

Except her serve. No matter what I said or how hard she tried, her serve was stuck.

I knew exactly what the problem was: She was "pancaking" the ball—pushing forward with an open racket face—instead of swinging up and out. "Swing like you're throwing a ball," I must have said a hundred times. When that didn't work, I'd demonstrate it myself.

"Ohhh, *now* I get it!" she'd say. Then pancake it just like before.

Finally, probably because I'd run out of ideas of what to do, I took her arm in my hands and moved it through the correct swing path. (I asked first. Anytime I put my hands on a student, I ask permission. It's a good policy that I suggest all coaches follow.)

And *voila*—she got it. Explaining it hadn't worked, demonstrating hadn't helped, but *feeling* the correct movement for herself finally allowed her to execute it. She'd experienced a breakthrough.

It was a breakthrough for me, too: Finally, I understood what I should have all along—that every student learns differently, and that what works great for Donna and David won't necessarily work for Denise.

If you're trying to get better at tennis, one of the most important things you can do is figure out how you learn best. Broadly speaking, there are three styles of learning. It could be that one style will help you in one situation and another will help you more easily learn something else.

Visual Learners need to see technique demonstrated. This can be live or on video. Slow-motion video is particularly helpful for these players.

Auditory Learners prefer to have ideas explained—particularly through analogies. One of my colleagues, Kevin Garlington, has come up with some great analogies over the years. One of my favorites describes the first step players take to their right or left to receive an incoming ball. Students are often confused when it comes to this first step—they've heard phrases like "drop step" and "outside leg pivot" but don't actually know what to do. Kevin says, "Pretend there's someone standing next to you. What would you do if you wanted to shake his hand?"

Eureka! Without any thought, the student turns to her right or left to "greet" the imaginary person. She's also learned how to take that first step to a ball that's hit to her right or left. Analogies work when they take a movement you already know how to do and apply it to a movement you're trying to learn. They bridge the gap between current habits and new skills you'd like to master.

Kinesthetic Learners need to physically feel a movement in their bodies before they can do it. They especially benefit from executing movements in slow motion and freezing at various checkpoints along the way. These freezes "pin" the muscle memory into their minds.

How do *you* learn best? In a moment, I'll provide an exercise to help you find out.

First, though, I want to make an important point about learning styles:

In my opinion, what's more important than figuring out your personal learning style is simply being aware that different styles of learning exist. When learning a new technique, players often give up too soon, not realizing that they could easily master it if only the information and training were presented in a different way.

TAKE ACTION

These next two assignments help you explore the concept of learning styles. Most people learn best through a combination of all three styles. Utilizing all three also makes the learning process more enjoyable by providing a richer, more complete experience.

Progression 1

Players: In your tennis journal, write about two breakthroughs you've experienced (they don't have to be related to tennis). For each breakthrough, how was the information conveyed to you? What allowed you to finally get it? Was the information conveyed the same way in each situation, or differently?

Coaches: Consider two students whose learning styles clearly differ. What clued you in to the fact that they learn differently? Given what you know about how each person learns, how might you teach the same technique to each student?

Progression 2

Pay attention to future breakthroughs you might experience. When they happen, write down the circumstances. Can you reverse engineer what caused the breakthrough to happen?

Progression 3

When Roger Federer hits a gorgeous drop volley that flutters delicately over the net like a rose petal dropped into a meadow of grass, we say that he has great "touch," incredible "feel."

Most players assume "touch" is some magical quality you're born with or without. But touch isn't magical. It's simply the ability to absorb the energy of an incoming ball instead of adding to it. Like all tennis skills, it can be practiced and learned.

The following exercise will teach you touch in the three different ways we talked about—visually, audibly, and kinesthetically. The end goal is that you'll be able to "catch" a tennis ball on your racket. You'll never do this in a match, but it's a cool trick that will impress your friends, make you look like a pro, and help you figure out which style of learning suits you best.

Drill: "Catch the Ball"—See It, Hear It, Feel It

In this drill, you're going to toss a ball two to three feet above head height, about an arm's length in front of you. Just before the ball drops past waist height, you'll "catch" the ball on your strings, smoothly and seamlessly, as seen in this video:

To pull this off, the racket needs to drop at the same rate as the ball. Then you scoop under and delicately catch the ball on the strings. If racket doesn't come down at the right speed, or if the "catch" happens too abruptly, you'll know it—the ball will have a harsh collision with the strings, will rattle around on the face, and might even bounce away.

Here's how each learning style would approach the drill:

Visual Learners: For you, what you see is what you get—so your first step is to watch and learn. Take a look at the video I mentioned above and pay close attention to how ball and strings stay aligned as the ball and racket descend. Watch how ball and strings meet—note how racket absorbs ball, delicately. Finally, watch for signs of success: If you see the ball bounce even once, you've still got work to do. When the drill is done perfectly, the ball should simply come to rest on the strings, like it'd been caught on a pillow.

Auditory Learners: For you, it's all about what you hear and how you hear it. You'll succeed to the extent that the explanation itself makes sense, typically with a metaphor. So: it's as if you're catching a water balloon—the way you instinctively pull your arms toward you as the balloon approaches and then gently cradle it in soft, spongy hands when the balloon arrives. Or—here's a crazy one—imagine catching a falling tennis ball in a piece of tinfoil. If you just hold the tinfoil open, the ball would rip right through. But if you lower the sheet of foil as the ball approaches, you could cradle it to a soft landing. Listening is also your cue to success vs. failure: listen for the familiar "ping" (or multiple "pings") when the ball hits the strings. If you hear this, you haven't succeeded yet. Your goal is to hear silence—no sound at all.

Kinesthetic Learners: You learn by *feeling.* So in this case, you want to pay attention to the physical sensation of collision or no collision between racket strings and ball. What you want to feel is *nothing*—"catching" happens when ball meet strings gently, in perfect harmony. Some other feeling-related sensations to aim for are *absorption, sponginess,* and *seamlessness.*

SECTION II

ON COURT

8

Effortless Power: The Kinetic Chain

The 2012 Australian Open final between Novak Djokovic and Rafael Nadal lasted 5 hours, 53 minutes—the longest Grand Slam final on record. In the fifth set, the two opponents were hitting the ball as hard as they were in the first few games— and with as much accuracy.

How did they do it? How do pro players hit as hard as they do, and for hours at a time, without getting injured or tired?

Advancements in racket and string technology have something to do with it. Same with fitness and post-match recovery.

But another reason—and the one that will benefit competitive amateur players the most—is correct use of the kinetic chain.

Simply defined:

The kinetic chain is the use of big muscle groups in the correct order, from the ground up, to smoothly deliver energy into the ball. It's the most efficient way to use the musculature that was given to us.

I consider the kinetic chain the most important technical factor in your development as a player. When you utilize it correctly, you hit harder, with more spin and accuracy, with less effort.

Because the kinetic chain is so important, I want to break down the definition and explore it in detail:

"big muscle groups" High-level tennis players rely on large muscles, not small, to create power. Large muscles include the upper leg (hamstrings, quadriceps, and glutes), the torso, and the shoulders. Because they're big, these muscle groups create more power for longer periods of time in a stable and reliable way. Less experienced players try to generate power with small muscles like the arm and wrist.

"in the correct order" To generate power efficiently, you need to use your big muscles in the correct sequence: legs first, then hips, torso, shoulders . . . and only then, in the final stage, your arm, wrist, and racket.

"from the ground up" The source of a tennis player's power is the ground. When you bend your knees and push your feet into the ground, you load energy in your legs—energy that can then be released with a wave-like effect up into the rest of the body.

What's the role of the arm in all of this? Not much. For the most part, the arm is simply along for the ride. The arm acts as a conduit for the flow of energy from the lower part of the body into the racket.

Using the kinetic chain to generate easy power is by no means unique to tennis. When a baseball pitcher unleashes a hundred-mile-an-hour fastball, we say, "He's got a great arm!" But what we should say is, "He's got great legs!"— because that's where the power came from, when he pushed off the mound. Boxers, golfers, NFL linebackers, volleyball players, and any other athlete who needs to transfer energy from his or her body into another object does so with the kinetic chain.

There's a good chance you've used the kinetic chain in your daily life, too. If you've ever had to push a sofa or some other heavy object across the floor, you wouldn't stand to the side of the sofa and push with your arm. You'd crouch down, load power into your legs, and then push forward and up.

To be clear: I'm not saying you couldn't hit a tennis ball

very hard using only your arm. But when you rely on your arm for power, three things result:

1. **Fatigue.** The arm, a relatively small body part, tires easily after repeated use.

2. **Injury.** Small muscle groups aren't designed for intense, repetitive movement. Nor can they withstand repeated stress. Tennis elbow (which is tendinitis) is a result of the repeated use of the arm to generate power. There's a reason you've probably never heard of a professional tennis player retiring due to tennis elbow. They use their bodies powerfully and efficiently.

3. **Lack of consistency.** Wherever the strings face at the moment of contact, that's where the ball goes. If you use your wrist and hand to try to manipulate the position of the racket at contact, you introduce tension into the swing. Tension leads to herky-jerky movement and an unreliable swing. The only way to achieve a smooth, repeatable swing is to keep the arm relaxed. Even on the volley—often a delicate shot that requires "feel"—it's the big muscles that do most of the work, allowing the small muscles to do nothing but absorb energy from the incoming ball.

A quick word about tension:

The kinetic chain is based on the idea that energy should flow smoothly through the body. It starts with your feet pressing into the ground and loading energy in your legs, and ends in a long, fluid swing in which all that energy is transferred into the ball. The only way energy can flow smoothly through the body is if you're relaxed. If there's tension anywhere, even someplace tiny, like your fingers, energy is choked off and your swing becomes choppier, slower, and more abbreviated.

Not surprisingly, a lot of my time on court is spent helping students to be less tense. When they finally begin to loosen up, they're scratching the surface of how relaxed they need to be to reach their full potential.

You might be wondering if there's such a thing as "too relaxed," "too loose."

I'll put it like this: In more than twenty years of coaching, I've never worked with a student who was too loose. Without even having met you, I can assure you that if you play below the 5.0 level, you've got too much tension when you swing.

I therefore encourage you to err on the side of "too relaxed." Start by loosening your grip on the racket: Hold it so that if it were any looser it would fall out of your hand. Don't worry—the racket won't go flying when you swing. At the moment of contact you'll firm up your grip involuntarily as you anticipate impact.

You may have noticed that I didn't mention the follow-through in this chapter. There's a reason: It's not an active part of the kinetic chain. The follow-through is something that should happen naturally when you utilize the kinetic chain correctly.

In chapter 11, "String Theory," I talk more about the follow-through and the importance of releasing the racket head—the idea that you let the racket go after contact. For now, know that the follow-through should be a passive movement, a result, and not something you "do."

In the online content for this chapter, you'll find videos that teach the kinetic chain step by step. You should also watch slow-motion videos of professional players. Notice how they use big muscles in the correct order, from the ground up, and how loose their arms are at contact. Pro players all have their own unique hitting style, but the way they all utilize the kinetic chain is the same.

The drill below will introduce you to the kinetic chain and how to execute it.

DRILL: The Kinetic Chain

GOAL: To show you what the kinetic chain feels like, so you can experience the flow of energy through your body from the ground up.

WHERE: In your home.

HOW:

Progression 1

Face a wall and stand eight to twelve inches back. Place both hands on the wall and push against it as hard as you can. Try to deliver as much force as possible.

Now do the same thing—except this time stand two to three feet back, crouch down, and *then* push into the wall. You'll be able to deliver much more force this time, because you can use the large muscles in your legs to push off the ground and channel force through your body into the wall.

Progression 2

Stand with your feet shoulder-width apart. Hold a tennis racket in front of you at shoulder height, parallel to the ground, with the tip of the racket in one hand and the butt cap in the other. This is your starting position.

Keeping your chest, arms, and racket exactly where they are, rotate your hips 45 degrees to the right. Again, your chest and the racket should remain as they were in the starting position—only your hips have moved.

Now rotate your hips back to starting position, then 45 degrees to the left.

Unless you're a salsa dancer, this movement might be hard for you to do! What you're experiencing is an essential element of the kinetic chain—a disconnect between the hips and torso, and the fact that they're able to move independently.

Progression 3

Begin in the same starting position, with a racket an arm's length in front of you in both hands, parallel to the ground.

Rotate your hips 45 degrees to the right, as before—but this time, allow your chest, arms, and racket to rotate afterward, as a result of being pulled by the hips. You should feel a stretch in your torso as you do this—it's because there's a very brief moment in which your hips are moving but your torso is not.

In this progression, you experience how the lower and upper body can work in a certain order, and how actively moving your lower body can deliver energy to your upper body without muscling anything.

9

There Is No Ball

I recently heard an interview with a famous golf coach. At one point, he was asked about his students' most common mistake. "They try to *hit* the ball," he said, "instead of just swinging smoothly and allowing the ball to be in the way."

I love how he phrased it—that the ball should just happen to "be in the way." It's a concept I've taught my students for years, except I explain it like this:

Swing your racket as if there is no ball.

I realize that sounds strange. What exactly do I mean?

Simply: As your racket approaches contact with the ball, *nothing about your swing should change.*

In other words, you do not "hit" the ball. You don't "snap" your wrist to impart spin on the ball. Nor do you suddenly rotate your hips, speed up your racket, or perform any other action in order to exert more force on the ball at impact.

Instead, you continue your swing—fluidly and effortlessly—as if there's no ball at all.

Before I explain why this is important, let's talk about where power comes from.

Whether it's a forehand, backhand, or serve, power comes from the coiling and uncoiling of the body from the ground up—the kinetic chain—*not* from swinging "hard." (You'll find a detailed explanation of the kinetic chain in chapter 27, "Serves II: First and Second.")

As it turns out, the hitting arm supplies very little power in a high-level swing. Instead, it's the coiling and uncoiling of the body that transfers power from body to racket to ball: When the body coils, energy is stored, and as you uncoil, that energy is released. Your arm just comes along for the ride to smoothly deliver that power.

I can imagine what some of you are thinking: *Sure, that might be true—but couldn't power also come from crushing the heck out of the ball? I mean, if I whack the ball as hard as I can, it'll take off like a missile, right?*

Actually, it won't. Because when you swing hard, two things happen:

The muscles in your arm tense. The tension starts in your fingertips and continues up into your wrist, forearm, biceps and triceps, and shoulder. All elasticity is lost; instead of being loose and stretchy like a rubber band, your arm is now stiff as a board. No elasticity means no efficient power.

Your body tightens. Anticipating a collision—even a small one with a fuzzy little ball—your entire body braces for impact. You do this unconsciously, which is why it's so important to train yourself out of it. When your body is tight, you choke the transfer of energy that *should* flow into your arm but now cannot. No energy flow means no power.

It's worth asking why we tense up in the first place.

As I see it, there are three reasons. First: your desire to exert control. In an effort to dictate the direction, speed, and depth of your shot, you tense up, believing (erroneously) this will help you direct the ball with precision. (Likewise, you fear that if you *don't* tense up, the ball will go flying over the fence.)

The second reason: instinct. Toddlers run straight into sofas and walls with abandon, but somewhere along the line they learn that collisions are bad and they should therefore brace themselves against them.

But the primary reason you tense up when hitting a shot? Physical panic. You want to hit a great shot, you want to *not* mess up, and to do this, you need to quickly execute a series of tasks (run to the ball, set up, swing, watch contact, follow through). Overloaded with so many demands, you revert to lockdown mode, panic, and tense up.

In any case, I believe this is the biggest difference between amateur players and pros. Amateurs fight hard against their own bodies, while pros allow energy to flow smoothly from the ground up, allowing their bodies to work *for* them.

One of my favorite drills relates to this idea of smooth, effortless power:

DRILL: There Is No Ball

GOAL: Powerful forehands and backhands with more fluidity and less effort

WHERE AND WHAT: On court, in the yard, or in your living room. All you need is a ball and an unstrung racket. (If you don't own an unstrung racket, I suggest you buy a cheap racket at a garage sale or Craigslist, and then cut out the strings. It doesn't have to be the same model you play with.)

HOW: Start with ten or so shadow swings (no ball yet) where you split-step, coil into a unit turn (lower body facing the net post, torso and shoulders turned to the side fence, racket back), and then smoothly transition into a fluid racket-drop and long, continuous swing that finishes over your opposite shoulder.

Keep your swing speed at about 25 percent of your normal effort. Focus on keeping your whole body as relaxed as possible.

Next, introduce a ball: Split-step and unit-turn like before, then drop a ball into your swing path. Do your usual racket-drop and swing. Because the racket has no strings, the ball will go through the frame, and your racket will continue over your shoulder.

If you're like 99 percent of the players who try this, you'll experience a strange phenomenon: a completely involuntary burst of acceleration and tension right when the ball would normally hit the strings. You can't help it! This brace-before-impact has been "trained" into you.

WHY THE DRILL WORKS: The purpose of the "There Is No Ball" drill is to train you out of this habit of tensing up at impact.

This is why we remove the strings but keep the ball: Pretty much every player I've worked with can swing a tennis racket smoothly when there's no ball to hit; few, however, can swing smoothly when there *is* a ball, because seeing that ball, and sensing the impending collision, causes them to tense up. When you remove the strings from the racket, you keep the ball in your swing path but take away the ball's ability to influence how you swing.

Do this drill enough (I recommend you do it every time you play, right before you step on court), and eventually your real-life ground strokes will feel smooth and effortless—as if there's no ball there at all. Believe it or not, this is what your swing should ideally feel like *every single time*!

VARIATIONS: As you get more comfortable with the drill, try it a few different ways. Alternate forehands with backhands. Incorporate movement—for example, you might split-step, unit-turn, move a few steps to the side, and *then* drop the ball and swing. Anytime we're challenged on the tennis court, our tendency is to tense up—which is why these variations are helpful.

An important point: Students sometimes ask me if simply being "self-aware" is enough to decrease the tension in their swings. If only it were that easy! But the truth is, our brains simply aren't powerful enough to do all the things required to hit a tennis ball *and* maintain the amount of focus needed to overcome an ingrained habit.

Which is why you have to train the habit out of yourself, physically, until a new, better habit is formed.

. . .

Next time you're out on court, try to generate power by *not* trying to generate power. Instead, swing like there's nothing to hit, no impact about to happen—the kind of easy, unhindered swing you'd have if there were no ball at all.

10

Good Feels Bad

Sometimes when I teach students a new and improved technique, they complain that it doesn't feel "natural."

"Good," I say. "It shouldn't!"

There's this notion out there that when something is good for you it should *feel* good. And that one way to know that you're doing something correctly is that it feels "natural."

Students expect that when they learn how to hit a forehand correctly, it will instantly feel amazing—that the skies will part, a beam of light will shine down, a chorus of angels will sing "*AHHHH,*" and their new forehand swing will feel light, easy, unblocked, and pleasurable. "Oh, so *that's* what a forehand is supposed to feel like!" they expect they'll say with relief.

But here's the thing: "Correct" and "natural" have nothing to do with each other.

Why?

Because when something "feels natural," it means one thing and one thing only: that you're used to it. "Natural" is an individual experience that has nothing to do with what's biomechanically correct. So when I teach a student how to hit a forehand and she says, "It doesn't feel right," what she's really saying is, "I don't like how this feels because it's not what I'm used to. I like my current habit better. This new one feels wrong."

"Good feels bad" is one of the most important concepts of tennis improvement (or improvement at anything, for that matter). The only way to get better at something is to create new, better habits. And creating new habits will always feel uncomfortable at first, even when it's good for you. A New Year's resolution is a perfect example. Waking up early to go jogging feels terrible when you first start doing it. So does eating carrots instead of candy bars. Both are good habits—but they feel bad because you'd rather keep on doing what you're used to.

This is why I'm glad when students tell me a new technique doesn't feel natural: It's a sign that they're doing something different from what they've always done, and that new, better habits are being formed.

Why is it so important that you understand this? "When you learn something new, it'll feel bad at first"—so what?

It's because if you don't understand it, you undercut your chances of getting better at tennis. Specifically:

1. **You might quit.** It happens all the time: A tennis player learns better technique, the technique feels "unnatural," so the student goes back to whatever she was doing before, without giving the new way a chance.

2. **You might assume you're doing it wrong.** You assume that one way to know you're doing something correctly is that it feels right. When it doesn't, you assume you're doing it wrong.

3. **You won't bother to learn.** If you assume that correct technique will inherently feel natural, you won't bother trying to improve with a coach or research on your own. You might think that if you do something enough times, your body will figure it out on its own, like a toddler learning how to walk. Here's the thing: Our bodies were designed to walk, but they were not designed to intuitively hit tennis balls. The best players in the world are great not because they have naturally good technique, but because they learned correct

technique when they were young and have been honing it ever since.

When it comes to tennis, there's no such thing as a blank slate. All of us, even children, step onto the court with a lifetime's worth of habits, as well as innate athletic abilities. So the first time you try a new and improved technique, fully expect it to feel uncomfortable. If you do the new thing right and it instantly feels easy, then treat it as a bonus. In my experience, it rarely happens!

So just because a piece of technique feels right doesn't mean it's correct. And just because it feels wrong does not mean it's not right. The only way to get better is to leave what feels "natural" and to do what's correct long enough until finally it, too, feels natural. You need to push through the strange until your body is retrained.

Are there certain improvements that usually feel good right away?

I can think of two examples.

The first is spacing to the ball. A lot of players set up too close to the incoming ball on ground strokes. When they create more space, they instantly feel freer and experience a more flowing and efficient swing. That said, the act of creating this extra space is going to feel unnatural at first, because they're used to setting up close to the ball. But the ideal habit—more space between player and ball—will usually feel better right away.

The second case is tension—specifically, getting rid of it. The minute you can get rid of all the tension you're carrying and simply allow the racket to swing freely, you'll feel good. Students sometimes say things like "Wow! I didn't know hitting a tennis ball could feel so easy!"

And yet: Because they're used to playing tense, the experience of playing relaxed will feel unnatural at first.

What's different about these two cases, however, is that players will immediately recognize the benefit of the new technique, even if it's different from what they're used to.

Before we conclude, I want to talk about the difference between "doesn't feel natural" and "hurts."

It comes down to one question: Does the discomfort linger after the shot? I expect that when a student learns a new technique, it might be a little physically uncomfortable at first; but if your wrist, shoulder, elbow, or anything else continues to hurt five seconds later, it's a sign that the technique is being done wrong. The movement might be correct. It could be you added tension to the movement in an effort to control or force it. This tension causes pain.

REFLECT

Progression 1

Think back on your tennis career. Find one or two examples of a correct movement or technique feeling wrong when you first learned it, but now you're glad you stuck with it and trusted the process.

Progression 2

Think of a time you quit on a new technique because it felt wrong. Are you willing to try to learn it again, even if it feels unnatural?

11

String Theory:
Let Go of Control

Throughout this book, I talk about the importance of *intention*—on every shot, you should have a target in mind (unless you're training a new habit) and a reason you chose it, even if you're hitting around with a friend.

But how do you hit targets? How do you make the ball go where you want it to go?

We can talk for hours about the importance of split-steps, unit turns, and how far your elbow should be from your body in the racket takeback. But ultimately, there's only one thing that determines where the ball goes: where the strings are facing at the moment of contact.

But here's the thing: The amount of time that the ball is touching the strings is four milliseconds. To put it in perspective, it takes you two hundred milliseconds to blink your eyes—the same amount of time as it takes to execute fifty ball strikes.

Four milliseconds is too short a time span for your brain to process. There's simply no way that you or I or Roger Federer or any other human being could actually *do* something at the moment of contact to influence the outcome of a shot. By the time you did, the moment would be long gone.

This doesn't stop players from trying. In an effort to control where their shots go and how the ball spins, players attempt to do many things at what they think is the moment of contact. They snap their wrist "at contact" to try to generate topspin. They manipulate the angle of their wrist to direct the ball in a certain direction. They clamp down and hold on to the racket as tightly as they possibly can to keep the racket in the position they think it needs to be in during contact; they're afraid that if they don't, they'll miss their opportunity to strike the ball correctly.

I've got news for you: No matter how quick and athletically gifted you are, you will miss your opportunity. You can't get your body to do anything during four-thousandths of a second. When you consciously *try* to direct your shots to a target, you decrease your chances of hitting the target. When you try, you flex your muscles and introduce tension into the swing. Tension leads to sudden, herky-jerky movement—the last thing you want if you're trying to send a ball to a specific spot. It also chokes off the flow of energy in your body and takes away your potential to hit with power and spin.

So how do you control where the ball goes?

By letting go of control. You choose a target, become "aware" of it, then strike the ball with a relaxed arm and a long, fluid swing, without trying to make the ball go there. After contact, release the racket head—allow the racket to continue along the path it's already on. This becomes your follow-through.

If you miss your target, it's because the strings were facing the wrong way at contact. To correct this, you adjust your timing. That means initiating the entire process a bit earlier or starting a bit later, so that the angle of the racket face will be slightly different when you strike the ball.

In my opinion, "ball goes where the strings face" is the most crucial, yet most neglected, concept in tennis. If players and coaches were to truly grasp it, it would change how tennis is taught and practiced.

Once players understand that accuracy comes down to where the strings face, they become aware of cause and effect. They begin to understand the physics of what's happening and the relationship between body, racket, and ball. It's now much easier to correctly adjust on future shots. They can work backward from their end goal—strings facing the right way at contact—and reverse engineer how to get there.

Consider what typically happens. A player hits a shot into

the net, then batters herself with a litany of self-criticism and reminders: "Bend your knees! Contact out in front! And take your racket back farther!" On her next shot, she might do all of those things, but if the strings are still angled wrong at contact, all she'll do is hit more aggressively and confidently to the same spot in the net. Instead of addressing the real problem, she's relied on a random assortment of clichés.

Just how accurate is "accurate"? If you set up a cone on the other side of the net, how close do you need to come to count it as a "success"?

It depends what level player you are. For players under 5.0, I consider anything within a six-foot radius of the cone as a success; within a three-foot radius as very precise; and hitting the cone directly or inches away as perfect execution.

You might think I'm being overly generous by counting anything within six feet as a good hit. After all, that's a very large target area—more than a hundred square feet. But consider this:

- The ball is on the strings for four-thousandths of a second.
- The difference in timing between a down-the-line and crosscourt shot is one-sixtieth of a second. A few blinks of an eye is the timing difference between a twenty-seven-foot spread in results.
- At contact, a difference in racket face angle of

5 degrees open or closed is the difference between a beautiful down-the-line winner that hits the baseline and a line drive that hits the back fence on a fly.

I'd expect higher-level players to hit the cone directly more often, and their success zone is smaller. Still, I'd consider anything within a three-foot radius as very accurate—an area of thirty square feet.

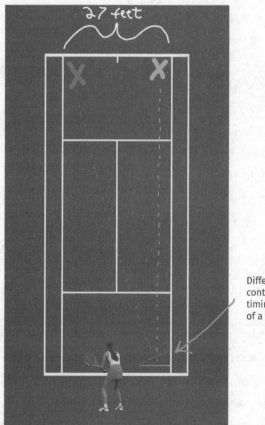

27 feet

Difference in contact point timing is 1/60th of a second!

DRILL: String Theory

GOALS: To train you to increase your level of accuracy by letting go of control.

To help you improve accuracy by adjusting your timing, instead of relying on movements in your wrist and arm.

To change your internal dialogue about what "accuracy" means.

WHERE AND WHAT: On court, with a bucket of balls.

HOW:

Progression 1

Stand on the service line, next to the doubles alley on your forehand side.

Your target is anywhere inside the doubles alley and past the opposite service line on the other side of the net.

Make a few slow, relaxed shadow swings. Allow the racket to swing as freely as possible, with no tension.

Now drop-feed a ball and swing exactly as before, slowly and completely relaxed.

If the ball lands in the target area, terrific! If it doesn't, don't alter your swing; change the position of your racket strings at contact by adjusting where you drop the ball by a few inches.

Drop it a little farther in front of you or a little farther back so that the strings meet the ball at the right angle.

For example, if you're right-handed and the ball lands to the left of the alley, contact was too far in front, which is why your strings were angled too far to the left. On the next swing, drop the ball a few inches farther back so contact is made with your strings angled slightly more to the right.

Continue to make these small adjustments until you hit your target several times in a row. Be sure to keep your swing long and relaxed.

How many out of twenty balls can you hit inside the target?

By the way—do you know how wide the doubles alley is? Most players guess two or three feet, but it's actually four and a half feet wide. Your target area for this drill is eighty-one square feet.

Progression 2

Place a cone, water bottle, or other target in no-man's-land on the other side of the court.

Stand at the baseline and drop-feed a few balls. Your goal is to hit the target using a fluid, relaxed swing. Do this by being *aware* of your target without actively trying to hit it. If you miss, adjust your contact point or angle of your strings open and closed.

Count anything within six feet as a success. Out of twenty shots, how many are successful?

WHY THE DRILL WORKS: The ball never lies. For this reason, good tennis players don't get angry when they miss their targets. They welcome the immediate feedback—feedback they can use to adjust. These drills give you instant feedback and objective data: Because neither you nor your targets are moving, you can focus on one variable—your contact point—and observe the cause and effect of tiny adjustments.

12

Practice Mind,
Match Mind

Have you ever wondered what Roger Federer thinks about as he steps to the baseline to serve?

Only the Fed knows for sure. I'll tell you what I think is going through Federer's mind as he puts up his toss . . .

TARGET

FOCUS

That's it. No reminders to bend his knees. No inner dialogue about how well he's playing or why he's not playing better.

Target and purpose. Aside from that, he's doing his best to keep his mind blank—not just on his serve, but during the entire point.

This is exactly how it should be for you, too.

What do I mean by target and purpose?

Your target is, obviously, the spot on the court where you want your shot to go. Your purpose is why. Are you trying to make your opponent hit a backhand, his weakest shot? Do you hope to receive a weak return so you can charge the net?

Together, target and purpose combine to create your *intention*—your overarching goal for the point. Before the point starts, you decide what your intention is, then you file it away and play the point. Your intention might be to pound away at your opponent's backhand until he makes an error, because you've determined it's his weakest shot, or to pull him off the court on his forehand side, so you can then hit an open-court winner. As the point develops, you'll need to improvise on your intention, depending on how well you execute and how your opponent reacts.

Intention is the only thing you should think about during a point. Whatever habits you walked onto the court with that day, those are the ones you use. Whatever you worked on in your last lesson doesn't come into play. Likewise, there's no focusing on all the technique-related stuff you're supposed to do; that's what practice is for. If there's one thing that will guarantee you lose a match, it's constantly thinking about technique. Conversely, you'll get much more out of your practice sessions when you focus on the process instead of the outcome.

The distinction between what you focus on in practice and what you focus on in competition is one of the biggest keys to tennis improvement. The underlying principle is this:

In practice, focus is internal: It's all about you.

In competition, focus is external: It's on the circumstances of the point and your opponent.

This is why practice takes place in a controlled environment: We remove variables and distractions so that you can focus as best you can on how you're executing—including the biggest distraction of all: "I want to win this point!" Only by focusing on yourself and what you personally are doing can you build new, better habits.

In competition, meanwhile, your goal is not to form new habits, but to win using the ones you already have. You do this by making your opponent as uncomfortable as possible—something you can do only if you pay attention to him, not to you.

What's the connection between practice and competition?

As my college coach used to say: The consistency of your output in matches is directly related to the quality of your focus during practice.

Notice he didn't say the "amount of practice," but "quality of focus." How many hours you spend on court has little to do with how well you play in a match. How focused you are in practice makes the difference. Most players practice with little or no focus. They mostly "hit around." If you want to improve, you need to practice with targets and goals—say, ten consecutive shots into no-man's-land. As you get better, decrease the target size and increase the goal (twenty crosscourt shots into no-man's-land). You should constantly test yourself to see where your limits are, then challenge yourself to go beyond.

TAKE ACTION

Experience the difference between internal and external focus.

Set aside one hour to hit with a partner. After a five-minute warm-up, spend fifty-five minutes on focused practice, as follows:

- Ground strokes past the service line: ten minutes
- Crosscourt and past the service line: ten minutes (five minutes each, deuce and ad court)

- Down-the-line and past the service line: ten minutes (five minutes each line)

As you practice, focus on *you:* Concentrate on what you need to do to hit your targets and execute your shots correctly.

Then spend the remaining twenty-five minutes playing drop-feed points (no serve)—first to eleven wins. As you play, think only about your intention—your target and purpose. Put your focus on your opponent and the circumstances as they develop.

REFLECT

How easy or hard was it to stay focused? When you practiced, were you able to focus only on yourself, or did part of you want to "beat" your opponent?

Once you started keeping score, did you stay focused on your opponent, or did you start to think about technique? Quick technique reminders are totally fine during a match. But during the point itself, your focus needs to be squarely on your opponent, your target, and your intention—not on how to execute.

13

Lessons or Tournaments?

If you want to win more at tennis, should you take lessons, or compete in as many tournaments and matches as you can?

Players are split into two camps:

At one end are those who believe that lessons are the solution to everything. When they lose a match, the first thing they do afterward is book a lesson so they can fix all the technical mistakes that were responsible for the loss. For these players, it's not enough that they hit the ball "in"; they want to know they're doing it correctly (and that they look good doing it).

Unfortunately, players who think lessons are the be-all and end-all of tennis improvement get three things wrong. First, when you lose, it's most often because of poor shot selection and bad (or no) tactics, not poor technique. Second, performing well in a lesson does not necessarily mean you'll play well in a match—once the pressure kicks in, your mind will be too occupied to rely on the new technique you just learned. Third, there are certain things that are best learned in a real match, like mental toughness and how to execute when it matters and you're on your own. No amount of lessons will make you a master of those things.

At the other extreme are players who *only* play matches. These players think lessons are a waste of time. They generally don't care how graceful they look when they hit their shots or whether they're technically correct in doing it. All that matters is that they win the point. They think the best way to become better is by competing as often as you can— that way, you learn how to execute under pressure and how to adjust your game from one opponent to the next. On this, they're right—your strokes and technique are only as good as they are on match point.

That said, if all you do is play matches, you'll never make big jumps in level. You'll go on defeating those players you can already beat, and lose to the ones who beat you now. Your technical skill set will remain stagnant.

Bottom line: To reach your maximum potential as a tennis player, you need lessons *and* matches. Either on its own will take you only so far.

. . .

What if you're just starting out—should you take lessons right away? Or should you develop a few fundamentals on your own, then dive in with competitive play to determine whether lessons would be worthwhile?

My feeling on this is clear: Take lessons now, as early as you can in the process. Here's why I'm adamant:

Beginning students often feel they're not "ready" for coaching. They're afraid that if they show up without knowing anything, they won't be coachable and the lesson will be a waste of money and time. So they resolve to get at least somewhat good on their own—that way, the coach will have something to work with.

I understand the logic. Lessons are expensive, and if you're going to invest the money and time, you want to be sure you'll get something out of it.

If there were no such thing as muscle memory, then waiting until you're "ready" would make sense. But muscle memory *does* exist, and it's powerful. From the moment you start hitting tennis balls against a wall, you begin to form habits. A significant part of my time as a coach is spent helping students unlearn habits that have been ingrained over the course of decades. Then we start building new ones. And even then, a lot of our effort is spent bringing awareness to the old habit when it rears its ugly head, which it does again and again.

On those rare occasions when I've worked with a pure beginner, meanwhile, the process is usually much quicker, because there are no old habits standing in the way. It's like the difference between learning French and learning French after you're already fluent in English—the grammar and vocabulary from your mother tongue will constantly get in the way. For this reason, the most challenging teaching situation is often when I work with players at levels 4.5 or higher. You might think they'd be the easiest to work with because they're already so good, but it's the opposite—their habits are so deeply ingrained that taking them to the next level requires an enormous amount of work from both of us.

I therefore strongly suggest that if you're a beginner, or if you're returning to the game after a long time away, invest in solid instruction now, on the front end. To make sure you're "ready," familiarize yourself with the different strokes and grips, and watch slow-motion videos of the pros in action to get a sense of what high-level play looks like. Otherwise, show up for your lesson as a blank slate.

I want you to know I'm keenly aware that tennis lessons are expensive and that not everyone can afford them. The good news is that thanks to the internet, tennis players have a treasure trove of instruction and insights available at their fingertips—more than the greatest players of previous eras ever had. One of the main reasons I started Essential Tennis was to make high-quality tennis instruction available to everyone. By no means am I the only coach doing this—there are several other high-level coaches who provide quality instruction for free.

If you can't afford lessons, or if you can't find a coach who uses methodical, step-by-step progressions to build new habits the way I advocate, you can learn high-level technique and strategy on your own using only free online instruction. If you own a smartphone, you also have a slow-motion video camera in your pocket—an essential tool when it comes to evaluating your progress. Between those tools and what you're learning in this and other books, you can teach yourself to play tennis at a high level. My one piece of advice is that you experiment with a few online coaches, then pick one who resonates strongly with you and stick with him or her. This way, you won't get confused between slight variations in their philosophies, and you'll have one clear track for progress.

REFLECT

In your tennis journal, think about two tennis skills you currently lack but want to develop—one that's better suited to improving through instruction, and the other that you can learn only in a match.

Then follow through on each: Book a lesson or set aside time to research the first skill online, and schedule a match in which you'll consciously try to work on the second.

14

Do(n't) Copy the Pros

Search "hit forehand like Nadal" on the internet, and you'll get more than eight hundred thousand results. Almost fifty thousand of them are videos, many of which purport to teach you, step by step, how to hit a forehand like Nadal.

I get the appeal. At nearly eighty miles an hour (on average) and with heavy topspin—more than fifty rotations of the ball *per second*—Rafa's forehand is one of the best of all time. He's won twenty majors with that forehand, so whatever it is he's doing—from the extreme vertical swing path to the lasso finish over his head—we should do it too. So the thinking goes.

As a tennis coach, however, I strongly discourage you from

copying Nadal's or any other pro's style of hitting their serves and strokes. Here's why:

1. **What works for Rafa won't work for Serena . . . or you.** Every one of us, including our favorite pros, is built differently, moves differently, and is equipped with our own unique athletic DNA. Rafa happens to be a natural righty who switched to playing left-handed when he was twelve. Serena Williams's father, Richard, had her hitting tennis balls six days a week, for hours at a time, from the age of three. Their respective forehands work wonderfully for each of them but would never work for the other, or for you or me. All any of us can do is move our bodies in the most efficient way we possibly can.

2. **You can get hurt.** Most of us don't have the mobility or strength in our rotator cuffs needed to hit a kick serve like Dominic Thiem. Club-level players may not realize how much work elite players put into maintaining their bodies and expanding the limits of what their bodies can do, including flexibility, strength, and stamina. When you force your body to move in ways it's not equipped to, you risk serious injury. While I don't fault coaches for posting videos with titles like "Hit Your Forehand Like Nadal," I do wish they'd tack on a warning that it's for informational purposes only, and

that viewers might hurt themselves if they were to try it verbatim.

3. **You can't be sure what the pros' bodies are actually doing.** Even in slow motion, it appears that Federer raises both arms together on his serve, simultaneously. Only when you really slow it down do you notice that his dominant arm lags and that his racket points to the ground as he releases the ball. When you watch a professional player, even in slo-mo, there's a good chance you won't catch everything that's happening. The result is that you end up copying something that's not there to begin with.

4. **You can't distinguish between active and passive movements.** When Federer serves, his front (left) foot lifts ever so slightly off the ground. He doesn't lift his foot consciously, though; the lift happens as a result of how he coils back during the serve toss. Federer's foot-lift is what we call a *passive movement*—a movement that happens as a result of some other movement that came earlier. A player's unit turn on a ground stroke, meanwhile, is an *active movement*—a movement he actively performs as soon as he recognizes the flight path of the incoming shot. Tennis strokes are a complicated mixture of active and passive movements, and even in slow motion, it can be impossible to know which ones are which. Much of what you see in a high-level stroke is the result of movements you can't dis-

cern, either because they're too subtle or you don't know where to look.

Given this, you might wonder why the Essential Tennis website contains a library of hundreds of videos of the pros hitting ground strokes, serves, and volleys, many of them in slow motion.

It's because the best way to know what good technique looks like is to watch the most elite players in the world do it. What you should look for are the commonalities—those things that all the players in the Top 100 do. No two players on tour hit their forehands exactly the same way—not even the Bryan Brothers, who share the same DNA—yet all elite players turn their upper bodies early, lead the racket forward by turning their hips and shoulders first, and keep their head still at contact.

There are things I want you to pay attention to when you watch high-level players. These common movements are the ones you *should* copy. I've compiled a list of the twenty pro-level movements and habits that would most benefit amateur players, if only they'd incorporate them into their game. The fact that all men and women players in the Top 100 do these things is an indicator that you should, too:

1. Take smooth, fluid swings.
2. Fully engage the core, with coiling and uncoiling on every ground stroke and serve, to create effortless power.

3. Use the Continental grip to serve and hit volleys.

4. Utilize different grips for forehand and backhand ground strokes.

5. Employ the split-step.

6. Prepare early.

7. Keep your torso between your legs whenever possible to stay in balance.

8. Transfer weight into the ball when there's time and balance to do so.

9. Recover to the best possible position before the next shot is hit.

10. Attempt to hit the ball in the center of the racket.

11. Have intention for every shot.

12. Make sure your contact point is in front of your body.

13. Move smoothly and efficiently around the court.

14. Keep good distance between yourself and the ball.

15. Toss for the serve using your shoulder, not arm and hand.

16. Hit second serves with a heavy spin.

17. Use the kinetic chain correctly.

18. Be consistent in effort and intensity.

19. Use different technical tools to respond to different situations.

20. Work hard off the court to maintain a strong, flexible body.

15

Trick and Treat

If I want to help a right-handed player learn how to hit her backhand crosscourt, I could say:

> On this next one, strike the ball four inches in front of your normal contact point, and feather your wrist a bit more than you usually do so there's about a 125-degree angle between your right forearm and the back of your left hand. At contact, aim for a spot on the ball a quarter-inch left of center and 5 degrees below the equator of the ball—if the ball is a clock, try for 8:30. Then drive up and through to 2 o'clock with

full extension as 95 percent of your weight transfers forward onto your front foot.

Or I could say:

Hit this next ball into the side curtain on a fly.

Which instruction is easier to follow?

The second, obviously—even though I asked the player to try for an outcome she doesn't actually want.

It's one of my favorite teaching methods—"tricking" students into attaining a desired outcome by having them exaggerate the process of getting there. I call it "Trick and Treat," and it can be used to fix any part of a player's game (that part is *not* an exaggeration). If a student's forehand consistently sails long, I ask him to aim for the top of the net. To teach a player how to drive his backhand through the court, I'll ask him to swing down through contact.

If you're stuck in a rut, exaggerating the outcome you want will break you out of that rut immediately. Better yet, this approach can be used both in practice and in a match. As it turns out, exaggerations are more than just effective—they're necessary. Here's why:

When players learn new techniques, what's required are tiny adjustments. Believe it or not, players at every level are able to make these tiny adjustments; the problem is that small adjustments *feel* large, since we're not used to them. It's related to the phenomenon of biomechanical dissonance (chapter 3) and the difference between "feel" and "real."

Because tiny adjustments feel large, a player won't make the adjustment she needs to—she'll back off, afraid she's adjusting too far (even though it's just right). Instead, she'll make what *feels* like the right adjustment, but it'll be either much too small or, most likely, the exact same thing she was doing before—and with the same outcome. She'll then typically blame herself ("Uch, I'm terrible!"; "Why can't I do this?") and assume the problem must be something else ("My timing's off"; "I should try a lighter racket"; "I'm not able to hit crosscourt").

Often the solution is to overcorrect—and in doing so, to end up at exactly the right spot.

Here are some favorite exaggerations I've used with students that will help you improve your own technique:

AILMENT	EXAGGERATION
Ground strokes/serves go into the net	Aim for "long"—the back fence on a fly or the opposite baseline.
Ground strokes/serves go long	Aim for the top of the net, or even the bottom.
"Late" timing—ball won't go crosscourt	Aim for the side-fence crosscourt.
Can't hit down-the-line—ball skews to the middle	Aim wide of the doubles alley down-the-line.
Can't hit down-the-line—ball goes into doubles alley	Aim for center of the court.
Ground strokes land short	Try for extreme net clearance—ten racket lengths.
Kick serve isn't spinning	Swing up at 90 degrees and parallel to the baseline.
Ball toss sails over and behind head	Toss to an "air target" five feet in front and to the other side of you.

Can't hit topspin on your forehand	Swing vertical through contact, 90 degrees up—no forward motion through the ball at all.
No "touch" on volleys	At contact, grip the racket as lightly as you possibly can and don't move it—any less tension, and it would fall out of your hand.

What about during a match? Could you utilize exaggeration to recalibrate your strokes?

Yes—kind of. The difference is that in a match, you don't exaggerate nearly as much—I prefer to think of it as adjusting. Instead of aiming for the back fence to get your forehand deeper, aim for the baseline or just behind it. In a match, the overcorrection should ideally remain within the parameters of the court.

The other difference is that in competition, you should stop overcorrecting as soon as you attain the outcome you want: You've recalibrated successfully, so no need to exaggerate further. When working on technique changes, meanwhile, you should continue to exaggerate, even after you attain whatever goal you're striving for, as a way to internalize the "feel" of your new swing. Returning to the example at the start of this chapter: Once my student successfully hits her backhand crosscourt into the curtain, I'd have her hit twenty to thirty more in the same way, then slowly work her back to where she's aiming for a target inside the court. That same process can be used for every other exaggeration listed above.

DRILL: Trick and Treat

GOAL: Achieve precision on ground strokes and serves by exaggerating the angle of the racket face at contact.

WHERE AND WHAT: On court, with a partner, coach, or ball machine; or on your own if you're working on your serve.

HOW: Choose an outcome that you might achieve through exaggeration—perhaps hitting your serve in the far back corner of the service box, or hitting your backhand down-the-line.

In order for exaggeration to be most effective, you should work off the same incoming ball every time, so have your partner, coach, or ball machine feed the same ball to the same spot.

Attempt to achieve your goal by exaggerating the outcome on at least twenty shots. Then gradually pull back, from extreme outcome to the real one.

WHY THE DRILL WORKS: By exaggerating the outcome, you "trick" yourself into deviating from your current habit to a new one.

TAKE ACTION

Progression 1

List five of the most common errors and miscalculations you tend to make in a match—everything from hitting your slice into the net to hitting down-the-line (riskier) instead of cross-court (safer). Now come up with one exaggeration you might use to correct for each.

Progression 2

Play a match. Make a conscious effort to recalibrate as you go along by using the exaggerations you came up with in Progression 1. When you're first learning how to use exaggerations, you might recalibrate between points ("On the next point, I'll hit my forehand with a lot more net clearance"). As you get better at it, you can exaggerate during points, as the point unfolds, by paying attention to where your previous shots land relative to where they should be.

16

Pushers I: Shape

One of the most popular digital instruction programs I've created is called "Pusher Domination."

If you're not familiar with the term, a pusher is someone whose only strategy is to "push" the ball back—usually in a slow, loopy arc. For this reason, players should look forward to playing against pushers—they don't challenge us with power or spin, and their returns practically beg to be crushed. Instead, pushers are reviled. Their slow, arching returns drive players crazy. Their purely defensive playing style is dismissed as "not real tennis."

Why would this be? What makes pushers so annoying to play?

In a word: They win. It turns out that their strategy—"just get the ball back"—is surprisingly effective. What's worse is that because they don't hit hard, we expect to beat them, and when we don't, we're humiliated.

There is one surefire way to beat pushers; I explain how below. But first I want you to understand why they win as often as they do.

As I reiterate throughout this book, tennis is a game of mistakes: The winner of any given match is the one who does a better job of making the other player screw up.

Pushers are phenomenal at this: Their slow, loopy returns induce tons of errors from their opponents. The reason is that most players below the 4.5 level share a common weakness: They can't play reliable offense. They can hit hard, or they can hit with consistency, but they can't do both at the same time.

As a consequence, when a pusher hits a slow, high-arcing ball, the average player *wants* to crush it, and knows he *should* crush it, but he can't. Instead, he does one of three things:

1. **Overhits.** He tries to smash the easy sitter—but he doesn't know how to supply power correctly, so the ball sails long or goes straight into the net.
2. **Pulls back.** Not confident he can hit the ball hard and keep it in, he decelerates his swing and either

hits the ball into the net or taps back a weak return that the pusher will then easily push back.

3. **Mentally crumbles.** Frustrated he's messing up on such "easy" shots, the player loses concentration and mentally checks out.

How can I make such a blanket statement that the majority of players below 4.5 can't play reliable offense?

Well, if they could, they wouldn't be stuck below 4.5. A big difference between them and 4.5+ players is that the latter are able to hit aggressively with consistency.

So the first half of how to beat a pusher is: Learn how to hit offensively and get it in.

The second part of the solution is mental—specifically, not getting flustered with the pusher's style of play and the errors he causes you to make.

I suppose I could end the chapter there: "To beat a pusher, hit aggressively with consistency and don't get upset."

But how do you do these things?

Let's talk about the mental side first. The best way to keep your sanity when playing pushers is to *respect* them. The minute you recognize that simply pushing the ball back over the net is a legitimate way to win, you won't feel so annoyed. One great way to start is to stop calling them "pushers" and instead call them "grinders" or "defensive specialists," as a way to remove the stigma.

As for how to play reliable offense:

Hitting with power and consistency comes down to utilizing what's known in the tennis world as "shape."

Shape is the amount and type of curve on the path of your shot. A shot that has "good shape" leaves your racket on an upward trajectory at high speed, arcs over the net with plenty of clearance, and then dips down into your opponent's court. When a pusher hits a slow, arching shot that lands near the service line, that's not shape. Shape is characterized by an arc and pace controlled by intentional spin, as opposed to relying on gravity alone.

To achieve shape on a ground stroke, you need to hit the ball confidently with topspin. It's simple physics: When the ball rotates quickly end-over-end toward your target, the downward rotation creates a pocket of high-pressure air on top of the ball that pushes the ball down, back into the court.

What's great about shape is that it gives you the best of both worlds: power *and* margin for error (or safety). The arc-like trajectory allows for net clearance, and the topspin brings the ball back down into the court. You've eliminated two of the three ways you can make an error. (The third is hitting wide; the solution to this is to work on your timing using the drill in chapter 11 and choose safer targets away from the lines.)

The only way to hit hard with topspin is by using a vertical swing path. Coaches use various phrases to describe this; "swing low-to-high," "brush up the back of the ball," and (completely wrong) "hit over the top of the ball" are some of the more common ones. The first two have been so overused for decades that they've lost their impact. Hearing "brush up" for the 3,000th time isn't going to help you hit with any more topspin than the 2,999th. The third phrase is physically impossible: You can't make a ball go forward if your racket strings face down at contact and the ball isn't on the strings nearly long enough to massage the racket around the ball.

When teaching topspin to my students, I like to say, "Swing up and through." What's important is that at the moment of impact your racket needs to be traveling upward at least a bit, so that the ball will rotate end-over-end, as if it were rolling toward your target. The steeper the upward angle of your swing and the faster your racket is moving, the more topspin you'll create. Rafael Nadal creates more topspin on his forehand than any other player in history—more than 3,200 rotations per minute—and if you watch how he swings, you'll understand why: He swings incredibly hard at a very steep upward angle.

That said, Nadal is an outlier. Most pros swing up toward their ground strokes at an angle of 45 degrees on an average rally ball: They deliver an equal amount of energy upward (for spin) as forward (for power).

One advantage of topspin is that you can hit as hard as you want, as long as you have the correct racket path and racket face—the ball will always dive back down into the court.

Another is that when the ball lands on the other side of the court, it "kicks" up at a steeper angle. Your opponent will have a hard time returning this shot—we prefer to hit a ball that's in our strike zone, between our upper thigh and lower chest. Anything shoulder height or higher throws most of us off-balance.

At the end of this chapter, I'll share the drill I use to teach hitting with shape. First, here are other tactics you should use against pushers:

1. **Bring them to the net.** Pushers are happiest on the baseline, where they can scramble side to side tracking down your shots. They often neglect volleys and overheads. When you can bring them up to the net, you place them in unfamiliar territory.

2. **Move them forward and back.** Tennis players spend a lot of time trying to move opponents right and left, but the majority of players, including pushers, are most uncomfortable when forced to move forward and back. Do this by hitting alternately deep and short.

3. **Play your game, not theirs.** When playing a pusher, you might be tempted to "push back," with the hope that if you run him around long enough, he'll make an error. Doing this plays right into the pusher's hands. His strategy is constructed around chasing down balls forever until the other guy messes up, and he's great at it. You'll never beat a good pusher at his own game, unless it's also your own.

DRILL: Shape Up

GOAL: To teach you how to hit with "shape," so you can hit with reliable offense—power and consistency.

WHERE AND WHAT: On court, with a bucket of balls.

HOW:

Progression 1

1. Stand six to eight feet back from the net.
2. Hold your racket up at the very top of your grip with your dominant hand. Begin with the tip of your racket pointing down toward the court, your arm and hand relaxed at your side.
3. Execute a slow, smooth shadow swing as follows: As you swing, try to move the racket upward but not forward, and rotate the tip of the racket up in a half circle so that you finish with the racket pointing straight up, about an arm's length in front of you.

Progression 2

Same as above, except this time drop a ball an arm's length away from your body and a bit out front after Step 1, above.

Make a smooth, relaxed swing like before. Your goal is that at contact, the racket handle is parallel to the ground and the strings are parallel to the net—the approximate halfway point between your start and finish positions.

As you swing up past the ball, listen for a clicking sound—that's the sound of the strings moving against each other—and watch for a big curve as the ball leaves your racket at an upward trajectory.

WHY THE DRILL WORKS: This drill isolates the vertical component of the forehand ground stroke. This causes you to hit the ball with lots of shape—it's the low-to-high portion of the swing that creates the topspin.

VARIATIONS: Try this drill on the backhand side as well. If you hit a two-handed backhand, feed with your dominant (bottom) hand.

17

Pushers II: Over and In

If you could choose one of the following, which would it be?

a. Roger Federer's forehand
b. John Isner's serve
c. That every time you play a match, you'll be the last player to hit the ball over the net and in

It's a no-brainer: C. Pick that, and you'll win more Grand Slams than any other player in history and see your likeness molded into a statue outside the International Tennis Hall of Fame.

I have a feeling most players at the amateur level would pick A or B. It's just too enticing—to hit forehands like Federer, or to deliver 150-mile-per-hour serves that leave your opponents frozen in their tracks.

Truth is, neither of those things matters unless you can utilize the tools effectively. I encounter this phenomenon all the time—players who get so hung up on technique that they forget what technique is for. They want to hit harder, serve faster, smash overheads like a pro . . . but in their ruthless pursuit of these skills, they lose touch with why other skills matter: so that you can be the last player who hits the ball over the net and in.

There is, however, one group of players who haven't forgotten this: pushers. They're often dismissed as talentless hacks, their playing style as "not real tennis." But what if we tried to learn something from pushers and how they play? Is there anything pushers might teach us?

Yes. Three things, actually. The first being what we just talked about: Pushers never forget that the ultimate point of tennis is to hit the ball over the net and in one more time than your opponent.

The second thing pushers know is that *you should take only as much risk as necessary.* Most players do the opposite: They hit harder than they need to, and closer to the lines than they should, when they could just as easily beat that day's opponent without having to work nearly so hard or having to beat themselves in nearly so many points.

Compare that to pushers: They take on barely any risk. They just hit the ball back, high over the net and to the middle of the court, and let *you* take on the risk (like money managers who invest your savings in stocks and then charge you a percentage, whether the stock goes up or not). They realize that simply getting the ball back will often be enough to win the point—eventually, the other guy will make a mistake.

This leads us to the third thing pushers know: Tennis is all about making the other guy uncomfortable. Power, topspin, depth, lag, the kinetic chain—they're all used to make the opponent uncomfortable. There are plenty of ways to do that, too, like hitting the ball high and deep. If you can master the art of hitting high and deep, you'll win the majority of points by far against most players.

If you want to see effective pusher tactics in action, check out some YouTube videos of MEP—the Most Exhausting Player (his real name is Ben). He flew out to Milwaukee to play me, and he's played several other well-known online coaches and players. Ben is a 4.5-level player with 3.0-looking strokes. His mantra is simple—get the ball back, no matter what. He exhausts his opponents by running us all over the court, forcing us to return ball after ball until we're drained. He's also incredibly resilient mentally. A US Marine Corps veteran, he treats each match like a mission. He doesn't get down on himself for making mistakes, accepts that he won't win every point, is prepared to adjust when needed, and refuses to show signs of weakness. I ended up beating Ben by using the principles in this book, but, as his nickname suggests it would be, it was a big challenge mentally and physically.

To be clear: I'm not saying you should necessarily play like a pusher and hit the ball back with only minimal force and risk. If you do that, sooner or later you'll run up against opponents with the skill sets to beat you, and your development will halt.

Instead, pay attention to some of the tactics pushers use, think about why they work, and incorporate them into your game. A well-rounded tennis player has many qualities, some of which are characteristics of the pusher. My college doubles partner, Mark, is a perfect example. Mark is one of the savviest tennis players I've ever met—he exemplifies what's known as "big-picture tennis." He could hit hard, always with plenty of net clearance, without risking more than he had to. He knew when to dial it back and allow our opponents to make a mistake. Mark had lots of weapons, and he called on each one as needed.

TAKE ACTION

Next time you play a match, hit around with your opponent beforehand like usual—and as you do, consider how much risk you think you'll need to take on to beat him. Put an actual number on it, from 1 to 10—how aggressive do you need to be?

Hint: If you have better technique or footwork, are more

consistent, are in better physical shape, or appear more mentally tough than your opponent, then your required risk level is low. Play the least risky style of tennis required to win. Continue to reevaluate throughout the match and adjust as needed. Keep in mind that the harder and closer to the lines you hit, the greater the chance you'll beat yourself.

That's the essence of big-picture tennis: remembering that the ultimate point is to get the ball over and in one more time than your opponent, and doing that in the least risky way possible.

18

Ultimate Tennis Warm-up

If you have your own physical therapist or sports psychologist, and you travel to matches with a masseuse, I envy you, and suggest you skip this chapter—you don't need it.

If, however, you're like the rest of us—read on. We're going to talk about the best way to prepare for a match.

A proper warm-up will give you a fast start out of the gate and allow you to play your best, smartest tennis and stay injury-free. It has three components: mind, body, and strategy.

Mind

When you hear "warm-up," you probably think about all the things you can do to loosen up your body. But your first priority to get ready for a match is to prepare your *mind*. If you're a 4.0 United States Tennis Association (USTA) competitor, I can assure you that most of your peers do *nothing* to prepare themselves psychologically for a match. But if you leverage self-discipline, you'll put yourself at an immediate advantage, before you've even picked up your racket.

Your mental warm-up begins on your way to the court. The goal of the mental warm-up is to put yourself in your ideal mental state for competition. This means decluttering your mind of anything that could distract you, so you can play with full concentration and focus.

Here are some of the tools that will help put you in your ideal psychological state. Try them all, invent a few of your own, and see which works best for you.

a. **Music** is a great way to put yourself into your ideal psychological state. Some players prefer high-octane fight songs of the "Eye of the Tiger" variety; others do best with Beethoven, Bach, or Enya. One of my students created a pre-match playlist. She's got Cat Stevens, A Tribe Called Quest, and the first-act finale of *Les Miserables* on consecutive tracks—an eclectic sequence. The songs trigger fond memories and positive emotions, and put her in the mental space she wants to be in.

b. **Audiobooks and podcasts** can also put you in the right mental place. Brad Gilbert's *Winning Ugly*, Tim Gallwey's *The Inner Game of Tennis*, and the book you're reading now are all available as audiobooks. So are Andre Agassi's *Open* and Maria Sharapova's *Unstoppable*. These and other books will shift your mind from work/family/my-mother-in-law's-coming-to-visit to tennis.

In my *Essential Tennis* podcast, I talk about strategy, technique, and the mental side of the game. You can subscribe to it for free on your phone's podcast app. Other podcasts feature interviews with athletes and coaches from the world of sports, experts on achievement, and anything else you can imagine. Less important even than the actual content is that they put you in a state of mind that will allow you to perform best.

c. **Thinking** healthy thoughts—or not—will partially determine how you play. If you're nervous or doubtful, try *not* to push these negative thoughts away—in my experience, any attempt to micromanage thought leads to more anxiety. Accept that you're anxious and remind yourself why: because you *care*, and that's a great thing. Then reflect on the big picture, like how much progress you've made and how grateful you are to be playing a sport you love.

One of my students came up with a pre-match reflection she calls "Tenn-Us." As she explains it:

"As I drive to the court, I think about how someone, somewhere, took the time to design my racket, and that other people spend hours each day researching how to manufacture the very best kind of string. I think about the people who mixed and poured the cement that became the surface of the court I'm about to play on, and that someone hand-painted the white lines perfectly. All so that I and other tennis players can enjoy this wonderful sport."

d. **Meditation** is another way that millions of people are able to quiet their mental noise and cultivate inner peace. At various points throughout my playing and coaching career, I've used meditation, with great results. There are plenty of meditation apps out there, including "Headspace," "Waking Up," and "Insight Timer," which offer free, guided audio sessions.

Body

To properly loosen up your body for a match, you need to do a *tennis-specific dynamic warm-up*, in which you move as you stretch. This is as opposed to a *static* warm-up, in which you stand in place for thirty seconds and pull your arm across your chest. (Static stretches elongate the muscles and are ideal *after* exercise.)

The following dynamic routine will increase your heart

rate, activate your entire body, and mimic how you'll move on court. I demonstrate the entire workout online. You'll also find a PDF you can print and put in your tennis bag. I suggest you do the routine in the order I present it.

Finally—you don't need to wait for a court to become available to start your physical warm-up. This routine can be done between courts, at the wall, or even in the parking lot.

Legal disclaimer: Since I'm not a doctor or certified trainer, you should consult your physician before doing any of these exercises. And if you ever feel dizzy, ill, or experience pain while doing the routine, stop.

ESSENTIAL TENNIS PRE-MATCH WARM-UP

1. **Lower Body**
   - Butt-kicks
   - Knees-to-chest—walking or in place
   - Side shuffles
   - Grapevines: side shuffles with front and back crossovers
   - Forward lunges
   - Side lunges
   - Frankensteins, aka Tin Soldiers—walk with legs fully extended, fingertips touching toes.
   - Footwork—run a few patterns you're likely to use in the match, including split-steps in which you explode sideways and forward to the ball.

2. **Arms**
   - Arm circles—forward and back
   - Forearm flexes—hold your right arm straight out, palm down, and make a fist; rotate the fist clockwise until the back of your hand faces the ground. With your left hand, rotate your fist a bit farther so you feel a stretch, hold two seconds, then release. Do this ten times, then switch hands (rotate counterclockwise for left arm).
   - Wrist flexes—hold your right hand straight out, palm up. With your left hand, gently pull down on the fingertips until you feel a gentle stretch, hold two seconds, then release. Do ten reps, then switch hands.

3. **Jump Rope**
   A great way to get your entire body moving, increase your heart rate, and practice your split-step and "fast feet."

4. **Torso Rotations: Core and Kinetic Chain**
   This exercise imitates the way you utilize the kinetic chain to achieve effortless power. You can use either a medicine ball or a resistance band.
   - Medicine ball—begin with your weight evenly balanced between both legs and hold the medicine ball about a foot in front of you. Slowly coil back into a forehand unit turn, in which you transfer your body weight onto the back leg; then rotate forward to starting position, ball back in front

of you. If you're at the wall or have a partner, you can throw the ball forward after your coil. Do ten reps, then switch to backhand.

- Resistance band—if you prefer a resistance band (they fit in your tennis bag and are much easier to carry), loop it around a pole. Then face the pole and execute a forehand unit turn, pulling the band back as you load your weight onto your back leg. Do ten reps, then switch to backhand.

  Next, face away from the pole and drive your weight forward like you're hitting a forehand, as you pull the resistance band. Do ten reps, then switch to backhand.

5. **Hand-Eye Coordination**

While waiting for your assigned court to open up, don't just stand there—use the time to work on hand-eye coordination by doing the following:

- Juggle (learn how on the Essential Tennis YouTube channel).
- Racket taps—hit the ball up and down, aiming for the sweet spot in the middle of the strings.
- Frame hits—rotate your racket so the strings are perpendicular to the ground and hit the ball up and down off the frame. This will require precise hand-eye coordination.

A solid physical warm-up lasts fifteen to twenty minutes. If you were to do everything I listed above, it would probably take you a bit longer, so I suggest you pick the six to eight exercises that match your personal trigger points and address the parts of your body that need attention.

If you're short on time, you might be tempted to skip it altogether—but don't! You'll rob yourself of the chance to play your best tennis, and you'll risk getting hurt. Use the following warm-up to get loose in as little as five minutes. It shouldn't be your first choice, but it's better than nothing.

ESSENTIAL TENNIS ABBREVIATED
(FIVE-MINUTE) WARM-UP

1. **Lower Body—1½ minutes**
   - Butt-kicks
   - Side shuffles
   - Grapevines
   - Lunges—mix of forward and to the side
2. **Arms—30 seconds**
   - Arm circles—forward and back
   - Forearm flexes
   - Wrist flexes
3. **Jump Rope—30 seconds**
4. **Torso Rotations—30 seconds**
   With or without a medicine ball or resistance band

5. **Injury-Prone Body Parts—2 minutes**

   Spend the remainder of your time loosening up whatever body parts you're most likely to injure (back, legs, arms, ankles, or anything else).

Strategy

The third component of your pre-match warm-up is *strategy*. This begins during the hit-around with your opponent before you begin to play. The next two chapters talk in detail about strategy, but the gist of it is this: The purpose of the pre-match hit-around is not to assess how *you're* playing on any given day, but to assess how your *opponent* is playing—and then to put together a game plan based on what you notice.

The hit-around is also when you take note of potential distractions and external conditions that might influence play, such as wind, cracks in the court surface, how much running room you have on all sides, and chatty bystanders.

TAKE ACTION

Progression 1

Experiment with three new methods you've never tried before to help get yourself in a good psychological space before a match:

- Compile a playlist of music that puts you in the frame of mind you want to be in when you compete.
- Download podcasts and audiobooks.

- Find a big-picture tennis idea to focus on, like Tenn-Us, to widen your perspective and shift your focus off yourself.

Progression 2

Next time you play a match, make a concerted effort to prepare in all three areas—mind, body, and strategy. In your tennis journal, record the following:

- The music or recordings you listened to, and the degree to which they helped you feel mentally prepared.
- The movements and drills you utilized to prepare your body. Did you feel loose, limber, and prepared when the match began? Are there specific parts of the body you should have focused on more?
- Any distractions and external factors you noticed and how you handled them.

19

Against the Wind

The answer is blowin' in the wind.
—BOB DYLAN

I'm older now but still runnin' against the wind.
—BOB SEGER

All we are is dust in the wind.
—KANSAS

It's pretty windy out, so we should probably cancel.
—PRETTY MUCH EVERY RECREATIONAL TENNIS PLAYER

There's a reason so many artists sing about the wind. It's powerful. Invisible. And mysterious—you don't know where it's coming from or when it will strike next.

All outdoor sports are affected by wind, but none more than tennis—the ball is hollow, weighs a measly 2.2 ounces (about the same as twenty-five ping-pong balls), and spends most of its time in the air. In fact, a tennis ball is *designed* to be impacted by air—the ball is covered with hundreds of protruding fuzz pieces whose purpose is to grab the air around the ball as it sails around the court. It's no surprise that many players would rather not play at all if it's windy out. Who needs the hassle?

Personally, I think that's a mistake. Once you know how to adjust your game for wind, you can use it to your advantage. On a windy day, the winner is the player who adjusts most effectively. Here's how:

1. **Relax.** Many tennis players panic when it's windy out. The wind wreaks havoc on their game and accentuates whatever flaws they already have. But remember that the wind affects your opponent, too. Few players know how to adjust well for wind, so if you can, you'll have the upper hand.

2. **Identify.** Believe it or not, most players never bother to check which way the wind is blowing! They know it's windy out, and they leave it at that. Only if you know which way the wind is blowing can you adjust your game, so figure it out quickly. It's going to be parallel, perpendicular, or diagonal to the net.

3. **Adjust.** How you adjust depends on which way the wind is blowing. You'll need to do the opposite after each changeover. Here are the specific changes you'll make:

   Wind blowing toward you. When the wind's at your face, compensate by hitting harder and flatter than usual—otherwise, your shots will fall short. Keep your first serves hard and flat, and go all out on ground strokes—this is your chance to crank it. Your opponent's shots, meanwhile, are going to come in harder and deeper than normal. Adjust for these variables by keeping your home base a step or two farther back than usual, but avoid shortening your swing, since you'll need all the length you can get to fight against the wind's influence.

Wind at your back. In wind that blows from your baseline toward the net, your shots and serves will tend to sail long. Adjust by hitting with more shape—that powerful combination of topspin and net clearance that allows you to hit confidently and keep your shots in the court (chapter 16). When serving, opt for kick and slice. Incoming shots will arrive short and with less power—so be prepared to move in more frequently if you're comfortable playing net.

Crosswind. Wind that blows across the court pulls ground strokes and serves toward the sidelines. Even in perfect conditions, most players aim too close to the lines (anything less than four feet is very risky)—so, on windy days, you want to ignore an entire third of the court to be safe. Crosswind will affect your serve, too, so aim a bit farther left or right accordingly.

That's the simple part. What's more challenging is that incoming shots will drift either into your body or away from you. As soon as you identify the path of the ball, adjust your feet to allow for extra space or less space from the ball than you normally would.

Serve Toss

Many club-level players struggle to place their serve toss when playing indoors; if you're outside on a windy day, it feels downright impossible.

For this reason, I suggest you keep your adjustment simple. Depending on the direction of the wind, toss either a bit left or right, or a bit in front of or behind, where you normally do. One way to do this is by aiming for a different "air target." Or change your release point, as follows:

Crosswind blowing into your face: Release earlier. The toss will veer away from you, but the wind will bring it back.

Crosswind blowing into your back: Release later. The ball will begin over your head, then blow to the correct contact point.

Lengthwise wind blowing at you: Release with your arm a bit farther into the court. The wind will bring the ball toward you.

Lengthwise wind blowing toward your opponent: Release with your arm farther back than normal, even parallel to the baseline or behind it—the ball will sail forward to a better contact point.

Many players try to adjust by tossing lower, thinking the less time the ball is in the air, the less time there is for it to be influenced by the wind. I don't recommend this approach—the serve is all about rhythm, and once you mess with any part of that rhythm, the entire system tends to fall apart.

If you've never tried to adjust for wind before, it can be hard at first, especially because whatever adjustments you make, you need to do the opposite when you and your opponent switch sides.

In time, you'll adjust without having to think about it. Until that happens, you might follow this one very helpful piece of advice:

Talk to yourself.

Literally—as in, before each game, or even each point, remind yourself out loud of whatever adjustments you should make:

"Wind is left to right—so my target is the left side of the court. His shots will drift right, so I need to be prepared to move that way."

"Wind is at my back, so I'll swing more vertically on ground strokes for topspin and shape. And his shots will land short, so I might move in."

Self-talk like this will help you recalibrate. The initial result will be fewer mistakes. Eventually, you'll look forward to a windy day, because you'll be one of the few players who knows how to handle it. It'll be like having your own invisible doubles partner out there with you on court.

TAKE ACTION

Next time it's windy out, set up a match or hitting session so you can practice the above adjustments.

If you can't find a partner, practice alone. Serve from both sides of the court. Pay attention to how the wind affects your toss and where your serves land. Then practice hitting and receiving ground strokes with self-feeds. Toss the ball high so that the wind will affect it. Feed in all directions—left, right, in front of yourself and behind, so you're forced to adjust your footwork. Take notes on where your shots land.

20

Mini Tennis

A friend of mine, a tennis coach, won VIP tickets to a Broadway show. She got a backstage tour, met stars from the cast, then sat in the empty theater and watched the cast warm up. For a few minutes, they all stretched and went over notes. Then the dance captain led the entire cast through the opening number—an elaborate dance sequence with complicated choreography—in slow motion.

"It was the strangest thing," my friend said. "All these talented dancers moving in perfect harmony at half-speed, like they were underwater or trapped in quicksand. And you know what I thought about as I watched them?"

I shook my head.

"Mini tennis!" she said.

Her analogy was perfect. The best way to prepare for a complicated movement-based activity is to do it in slow motion first. Broadway dancers are among the best dancers in the world, so if anyone *wouldn't* need to rehearse in slow motion it'd be them—and yet they did. They saw the value of literally walking through every heel turn, pirouette, and plié, slowly and with purpose.

Mini tennis, done correctly, is much more than a way to get loose—it's your chance to walk through the choreography of your upcoming match or hitting session. As you do so, you get to review the fundamentals of tennis technique in a slow, focused, relaxed way, without the pressure of going all out to win a point.

If you're not familiar with mini tennis: It's regular tennis played on half a court at half-speed. Players stand behind the service line and rally, using long, slow strokes. The idea is to keep the ball inside the service boxes.

You should ideally start with mini tennis every time you practice or play a match. The best way to do something fast—especially something as complicated as a tennis stroke—is to first do it slow.

When utilized correctly, mini tennis helps you accomplish all three of these critical developmental elements:

a. **Get loose.** Mini tennis is a great way to get the blood flowing and your feet moving, to shake off the rust, and to recalibrate your strokes and footwork as you hit all the important check-points.

b. **Establish timing.** Timing is everything in tennis. We've all had days when our rhythm is off and the game feels impossible. Mini tennis helps you establish rhythm in a controlled environment. That's why I recommend you move exactly as you would in a match, complete with split-step, unit turn, racket-drop, fluid swing, and long follow-through.

c. **Practice control.** Power is great, but power without control is useless. Playing at slow speed on half a court forces you to control the ball. You need to hit the ball in the center of the racket with proper spacing between your body and the ball, minimal tension in your arm, and precise timing. This is why many players skip mini tennis—they can't control the ball and would rather not leave their comfort zone. It's also why mini tennis is essential: If you can learn to control the ball at slow speed on half a court, you'll be that much better at it under regular conditions.

Here are some commonly asked questions about mini tennis, and their answers:

When I play mini tennis, my shots always go long.
How do I keep the ball in the service boxes?

To play mini tennis effectively, you need to be extremely loose and swing with a slow, relaxed swing. If you're tight or swing too fast, the ball will sail into no-man's-land. Having the angle of your strings too open (facing up toward the sky) will also cause the ball to travel past the service line, even if you're staying slow and relaxed.

Does anything about my technique change when
playing mini tennis?

No—except for the speed of your swing. All other checkpoints remain the same as in a match: split-step, unit turn, swing path, and footwork. Aim for contact slightly ahead of you with your head still. Last of all, follow through completely—long and smooth, allowing the racket to finish wherever it wants to go.

This is where most players break down: They mistakenly think that because the swing is slow, there's either no follow-through, or an abbreviated one. One of the main reasons we play mini tennis is to experience swing speed and length of swing as two separate things, and to understand that neither has to influence the other. You'll know you're playing mini tennis correctly if you can swing slowly and still follow through long and over your shoulder without having to force it to happen.

What strokes should I practice during mini tennis?

Try to simulate a cooperative baseline rally, including fore-hands, backhands, and slices. If you're a doubles player warming up with your partner, you can add volleys, too.

How long should I play mini tennis before moving back to the baseline?

I suggest a minimum of two to three minutes of mini tennis before moving back; five minutes is even better. Be sure to hit a mix of strokes—forehand, backhand, and slice.

Once in a while, you might dedicate an entire practice session only to mini tennis. Use a decompressed red- or orange-level kiddie ball to slow the game down even more—it's one of the best ways to hone technique.

When will I no longer need to play mini tennis?

The myth of mini tennis is that once you're "good enough," you can forget about it. But the opposite is true: At higher levels, tennis players employ mini tennis more, not less. In college, we started every practice with mini tennis. I've attended some of the biggest tournaments in the United States, including Indian Wells, the US Open, and the Western & Southern Open, and watched the most elite players in the world play mini tennis before hitting sessions. I'll post a video of high-level mini tennis workouts in the online content for this chapter.

DRILL: Slow and Relaxed

GOAL: Long, extended follow-throughs that happen on every ground stroke, regardless of how fast you swing.

WHERE AND WHAT: On court or at a hitting wall. You can also do this indoors with a foam ball or red-level ball.

HOW:

Progression 1

Stand in place and swing your dominant arm forward and back, like a pendulum. Then slow down, so you're swinging half as fast but through the same arc. This is what a mini tennis swing is like: It has the same long, extended follow-through as a regular stroke but at slower speed.

Progression 2

Perform slow, segmented shadow swings, in which you stop at four checkpoints: takeback, contact point slightly in front of your body, full forward extension, and follow-through over the shoulder.

Progression 3

Slow, continuous shadow swings at 25 percent speed, then 50 percent speed. Swing smoothly through all three checkpoints.

Progression 4

Stand on the service line and drop-feed a ball after the racket takeback. Swing through contact with a long, slow swing (50 percent speed) that extends forward before you naturally follow through over your shoulder. Try to clear the net by at least a racket length, and with the ball bouncing before the opposite service line. In this progression, you're teaching yourself how to swing slowly and smoothly. Learning how to control your movements and the ball at these slow speeds will help improve your precision and repeatability at higher speeds as well.

> **WHY THE DRILL WORKS:** These progressions bring awareness to swing length, swing speed, and shot result without the pressure of having to keep a rally going with a partner. Removing the expectation of a partner is key to experimentation, familiarization, and becoming comfortable with this (and any) new technique.

> **VARIATIONS:** You can do this at a hitting wall using a red- or orange-level ball to slow everything down—this allows you to focus on technique without feeling rushed.

Be sure to work on your forehand, backhand, and slice. As you get more comfortable with the drill, drop-feed the ball farther from you so you're required to move.

.   .   .

Mini tennis can also be used as a sport in its own right to help you work on specific skills. Some of my favorite competitive mini tennis games include:

The Pyramid

You and your partner each set up a small pyramid of tennis balls about two feet in front of your service lines. Play mini tennis as described above, with slow swings and long follow-throughs. The goal is to knock a ball off the other guy's pyramid. Score one point every time you do, and the winner is the first to three points.

The Pyramid: Forehand/Backhand Only

Same as above, except you use only forehands or only backhands. This requires quick, nimble footwork as you run around the ball and space yourself correctly.

The Pyramid: Crosscourt/Down-the-line

In this version, you and your partner set up pyramids in the outer corners of your service boxes—either diagonally from each other, in which you hit only crosscourt, or opposite one another (down-the-line). This forces you to work on control and directional placement.

Increase the difficulty by requiring you hit only backhands or only forehands in each scenario.

Point Play to 11

Same rules as ping-pong: Each player serves twice until one player reaches 11 points by a margin of 2. Anything that lands outside the service boxes is "out," and no volleys—every shot has to bounce.

21

Find Love at the Net

I hear it all the time: "I want to get better at tennis, but I can't find a partner to practice with—all anyone wants to do is play a match or hit."

It's true: Most recreational players aren't interested in doing target practice or other focused hitting. I get it—for many people, their hour or two on court is the highlight of the week, a chance to escape the stresses of office and home and enjoy the sport they love. The last thing they want to do is to hit only backhands or feed balls to a partner. And why play tennis if it doesn't make you happy?

That said, if you really want to get better at tennis, matches and "hitting around" alone won't cut it. You need to hit with *intention* as you practice certain shots to chosen targets. This, along with progressions and drills, is the only way to create new habits and replace old ones.

Some of this you can do on your own with self-feeds, at a hitting wall or with a ball machine. But these exercises will take you only so far, because the environments are controlled. Similarly, an experienced tennis pro is comparable to a finely tuned ball machine: Both will provide you with exactly the level of challenge you can handle and not a bit more.

A good practice partner, on the other hand, will provide spontaneous and organic variation from shot to shot, forcing you to adjust and leave your comfort zone as you hone technique. Finding a partner like this is challenging, but not impossible. At the end of the chapter, I'll present you with ten ideas for how to find your "tennis angel." But before you start searching, it's worth asking if your current hitting partners might not be so bad after all.

One of the complaints I hear most from tennis players is that they don't want to practice with players who are "worse" than them; there's this notion that the only way to improve is to play with people who are better than you. As one student emailed me:

The guy I hit with doesn't use proper technique and doesn't try to. His shots are all over the place, some of them flat, some with slice, some with sidespin. Meanwhile, I'm trying to hit a correct forehand with timing, topspin, and body rotation . . .

To which I respond, "So what?" Unless most of your practice partner's shots are out or in the net, then who cares whether or not he does a unit turn or hits with a certain spin? If his erratic play annoys you, good! It means he's hitting the shots you're least comfortable receiving—which are the ones you need to work on most. Practice players like this are valuable, because they expose the weaknesses in your game. Don't dismiss them—seek them out!

What this hitting partner will *not* allow you to do, how-ever, is work on a specific skill in isolation. For that, you need a partner who's willing to help you groove a particular shot or movement over and over.

And of course, you'll help him or her, too. A healthy practice-partner relationship is reciprocal, nonjudgmental, and benefits both players. As for how to best utilize your time, I suggest you do the following:

1. **Cooperative hitting.** In cooperative hitting, both players gain from the rally—neither player tries do dominate. But cooperative hitting is more than just hitting back and forth. Each rally should ideally have at least one of the following three intentions:
   - **A pattern:** like crosscourt or down-the-line.
   - **A target:** all balls past the service line, for exam-ple, or only drop shots inside the service line.

- **A numeric goal:** ten, twenty-five, fifty, or more total successful shots or consecutive balls in a row.

    As you get better, you can combine two or three goals into one rally, like fifty crosscourt shots past the service line.

    In the online content for this chapter, I provide a downloadable PDF with my favorite coopera- tive drills and outlines for various one-hour ses- sions, called "How to Spend an Hour-long Practice Session."

2. **Playing slow.** By "slow," I mean two things. First, I mean that you literally hit the ball slower than you're able to. A lot of players only want to crank it—they think a rally is valuable only if you're play- ing the most aggressive version of tennis you can. But to make a technical improvement on one of your strokes, you should hit at 50 percent power or less. Why? Because swinging slow affords you the cognitive space to consciously control your deci- sions and movements as you play.

    The best way to play slow is with mini tennis, in which you use long, slow, purposeful strokes to specific targets (chapter 20). To really take it down a notch, use decompressed red or orange kiddie balls.

    The second meaning of "slow" is that you and your partner take your time working your way up to full speed, as opposed to hitting as hard as you can to all spots on the court straight out of the box.

3. **Hand-feeding.** If you find a partner who's willing to get down on one knee and feed you a basket of balls, you might want to get down on one knee and offer that partner a ring. All right, so maybe that's going a bit too far, but you get my point: It's rare to find a partner who's willing to hand-feed you balls so you can groove your technique, and if you find such a partner, hold on to him or her. Feeds are important, because they allow you to focus on specific goals in isolation, with most or all external variables removed.

Return-of-serve drills belong in this category, too: One player serves from the service line (not baseline) so the other can practice receiving powerful serves, then they switch.

TAKE ACTION

Progression 1

Set up a practice session with a player who you perceive to be at least one full playing level below your ability. Commit to the idea that you can always work on hitting the ball in the center of the racket and keeping your head still at contact.

As you hit, pay attention to what's least "fun" about hitting with this player or what challenges you most. These are the things you need to work on; they're not fun because you're not good at them yet.

Progression 2

Here are nine ways to find a dedicated practice partner. If you try them all, I guarantee you'll find a like-minded player to train with!

1. **Post a note at area clubs.** Even if you're not a member, most clubs will let you put up a note on their bulletin board. For best results, be specific: State what level player you're looking for, and make clear that you intend to do drills and cooperative hitting with the intention of improving.

2. **Investigate PlayYourCourt.com.** My friend Scott Baxter runs PlayYourCourt—to my knowledge, the largest database of recreational tennis players in the world. Membership costs "less than the cost of a can of balls per month," as the site boasts. Other dotcoms worth looking into: GlobalTennisNetwork, TennisBros, Tennisopolis, and TennisRound.

3. **Go to Craigslist.** Old school? Maybe. But people do find hitting partners on Craigslist, especially when traveling. Also check out Meetup.com for tennis groups.

4. **Call three (or more) teaching pros.** Pros interact with dozens of players a week, and they'll know ex-

actly which ones are trying to improve the same way you are.

5. **Hire a good high school player.** You'll pay them, of course—*and* speak to their parents first, to make sure they're comfortable with it. From the high schooler's point of view, it's a no-brainer—it's easy money and sure beats babysitting.

6. **Call coaches at local colleges.** This might not work at Stanford, but smaller colleges, even Division I, could connect you with a player or assistant coach who'd be willing to hit for an hourly fee. Lots of schools have club teams for players who didn't make varsity—these players would be happy to get paid to be on court, and might even do it for free.

7. **Use Facebook.** Post on your own page, on pages dedicated to tennis groups like the Essential Tennis Group, or start your own such page.

8. **Scout parks, clubs, and tournaments.** Watch people play and get a sense of who might make a good training partner. Then approach them after they finish and simply ask if they're into it.

9. **Call the directors of tennis at local clubs.** Directors field daily phone calls from people looking for matches, lessons, and hitting partners. Leave your name and contact info and tell them what level of player you're looking for.

Progression 3

Now that you've found love at the net, the next step is to make the most of your time together on court. Here's an outline for a one-hour practice session. You'll find templates for other practice sessions in the content for this chapter online.

1. 5 minutes: Short-court mini tennis at slow speed. Be sure to hit crosscourt, down-the-line, and to specific targets.
2. 25 minutes: Directional hitting: crosscourt, down-the-line (both sidelines), volley-to-baseline, baseline-to-volley, and volley-to-volley.
3. 10 minutes (5 minutes each): Serve returns, while the other serves from the baseline or service line. Use flat and kick serves.
4. 10 minutes (5 minutes each): Feeds, for whatever stroke each player wants to work on.
5. 10 minutes: Serve and return points without keeping score. Incorporate "corrections"—when players make a mistake, feed the same ball again so they can execute correctly.

22

Play Like You Practice: The Great Swing-Speed Conundrum

A few years ago, I spoke with a fellow coach about one of his players. "I was amazed at how hard he hit the ball," the coach said, describing their first hitting session together. "It's certainly not what I had seen in his matches."

I hear this all the time from students: "I hit the ball hard when I practice, but for some reason in a match I become a completely different player."

Why is this phenomenon so common? What's happening?

Actually, it's about what's *not* happening—namely, your swing speed.

Here's what I mean:

Whether you're practicing, playing a match, or hitting around for fun, the conditions are the same: The net's three feet high, the ball weighs a bit over two ounces, and the court's twenty-seven feet across (for singles) and seventy-eight feet long. You step onto the court with your same skills, history, and athletic DNA.

The only thing that's *not* the same is that when you play a match, there's suddenly a specific outcome you wish to avoid. Notice I said "avoid," not "attain"—after over thirty years in the game, I'm convinced that for most players, certainly at the recreational level, the fear of loss is a more powerful internal drive than the desire to win.

Whether you're motivated to succeed or to not screw up, the end result is the same: In an effort to engineer your desired outcome, you swing more slowly. You do this because you believe that swinging slowly will help you control your strokes. But it won't! Although your intentions are good, when you slow down your swing, four very bad things result:

1. **Tension.** Tense muscles lead to choppy, abbreviated strokes—the opposite of the long, relaxed swing you need to achieve efficient power.
2. **Loss of shape.** Decelerating your swing leads to less net clearance (or none at all) and less topspin to bring the ball back down into the court.
3. **Lack of commitment.** Swinging slower leads to careful, tentative play. Instead of confidently playing to win, you put your opponents in the driver's

seat and allow them to dictate the outcome of the match.

4. **Lack of challenge.** When you slow down your swing, you naturally hit the ball with less pace and depth. This puts less pressure on your opponents and gives them the chance to attack.

You might not even realize you're slowing down. The urge to exert control is so hardwired that you probably subconsciously slow down your swing speed without knowing it. The fight-or-flight part of your brain hijacks the part that's responsible for your tennis strokes, to the point where you become a different player in practice versus competition.

Maybe you are aware of it, and you don't know how to stop it: You *want* to swing as aggressively in a match as in practice, but the fear of screwing up is so ingrained that you can't stop your body from slowing down your swing.

Given that this fear's so powerful, and that you might not even be conscious of it, is there hope you might fix it?

Yes. The solution has two parts, one of which is logical, the other completely counterintuitive.

The first half of the solution is that when you're playing a match, you need to consciously swing as hard as you do in practice. The operative word here is "consciously"; if you don't do it consciously, you'll likely subconsciously swing slower, even when you don't want to.

The second half is the part that's counterintuitive: You need to swing aggressively *in a direction other than your target.*

For ground strokes, this means swinging the racket at an increased upward angle, even though your target is ahead of you. On a serve, it means swinging up and out, along the baseline, even though the service box is forward and down.

This upward swing path gives your shots "shape." Hitting with shape allows you to clear the net and keep the ball in the court, without sacrificing the level of challenge you present to your opponent or needing to slow down your swing.

That's how experienced players solve the great swing-speed conundrum: by swinging as aggressively as they can control but in a different direction. Inexperienced players, meanwhile, do the opposite: Instead of swinging with the same speed in a different direction, they swing in the same direction but with a different (slower) speed.

In chapter 16, I teach you how to hit ground strokes with shape; in 27, I teach the up-and-out swing path needed for aggressive second serves.

Here, I'll share a drill that will help get you in touch with your swing speed.

If you want to swing as aggressively in a match as you do in practice, the first thing you need to do is be aware of how fast you're swinging on any given stroke. Most players have no idea! At most, they can say something like, "On that last one, I didn't swing as hard as I could have." But they have no incremental scale to work off of, no way to compare how fast or slow one particular swing is relative to another.

DRILL: Know Thy Racket Speed

GOAL: To teach yourself awareness of different gradients of speed, so that you can perceive how fast or slow you're swinging on any given swing.

To feel the relationship between input (effort) and output (racket head speed).

WHERE AND WHAT: On court, alone, with a bucket of balls.

HOW: Stand on the baseline and hit five serves (deuce or ad court) using 40 percent of your maximum possible effort— just below half-speed, what I call a 4-out-of-10 swing.

Now hit five more, this time using 60 percent of your maximum effort (6 out of 10).

Now hit five at 8 out of 10.

Finally, hit five serves at 10 out of 10: Utilize *maximum effort* to swing as aggressively as you possibly can.

As you make your way up the effort scale, pay attention to the difference in *feeling* between each increment. Can you sense the difference between a 4 and a 6 out of 10? If I asked you to swing at effort-level 8, could you do it without going all out?

Now do the entire drill again, except this time notice how fast the ball travels at each level of effort. At what number out of 10 did the ball travel fastest?

When I do this with students, I sometimes use a racket sensor. The sensor records data on swing speed and ball velocity. One very big discovery most students make is that they aren't capable of swinging at different speeds, at least at first: They *believe* they're swinging harder at 6 out of 10 than at 4 out of 10, but the data reports a swing speed that's essentially the same. It takes several repetitions before a student can adjust from a 4 out of 10 to an 8 of 10 and have the difference in swing speed be anywhere close to double.

It's yet another example of how hard it is to perceive the difference between "feel" and "real." What we experience in our bodies doesn't necessarily match what's actually happening.

A second big surprise is that maximum ball velocity almost never occurs with 10-out-of-10 effort. Instead, the ball goes fastest at effort level 8 out of 10—hitting with 80 percent of potential effort.

Why?

Because swinging harder than 8 causes us to tense up and "muscle" the ball. This chokes off energy flow and decreases the amount of power transferred into the ball. Again, the lesson is counterintuitive: To exert maximum power, you need to swing with a bit less than your maximum effort.

As it turns out, most athletes, even at the highest level, aren't able to transfer 100 percent of their energy into the ball. Even Nadal, who swings as hard as anyone, doesn't use 10-out-of-10 effort on most swings; he's probably at 8 or 9 on his most aggressive shots. Tennis is a game of errors, and going all out causes players to tighten up and make mistakes—even Nadal. Obviously, the pros can swing harder than we can. But another thing they do better is being aware of the maximum speed with which they can swing without getting tight.

> **WHY THE DRILL WORKS:** By adding effort incrementally, you feel the difference in swing speeds. You then discover that you *are* able to control how fast you swing on any given stroke.

NEXT STEPS

Find the highest number out of 10 that you can swing without getting tense. Once you've found your place on the scale, hang out there for a bit. Hit a bunch of balls at this effort level. Be attuned to what it feels like—the sensation in the body of being able to move freely.

After a while, take it up a notch and swing a bit faster. What happens to your body as you exert more effort?

This stage of the drill is meant to help you stretch your ability to accelerate the racket while remaining relaxed. Many beginning players can't swing more than a 4 or 5 without sabotaging their swing mechanics; Serena Williams and other pros, meanwhile, can swing at 8 or 9 over and over without sacrificing a thing (even though Serena's 9 is *way* more aggressive than yours or mine).

This kind of awareness and performance training is the bridge between swinging at a 5 with consistent looseness and control and swinging at a 7 or 8 with the same amount of fluidity.

VARIATIONS

Try this drill with ground strokes. It's easiest with a partner or ball machine, but you can self-feed, too. It's the same idea: Hit a forehand with 40 percent effort, then 60 percent, 80 percent, and so on. Feel the difference in your body between each swing. Also, pay attention to how fast the ball travels on each shot.

As for that coach I mentioned at the start of the chapter . . .

That was Todd Martin—former World No. 4, US and Australian Open finalist, and, as of this writing, president of the International Tennis Hall of Fame.

The player he'd been hired to coach? None other than Novak Djokovic—at the time ranked No. 3 in the world. When he and Todd started working together in 2009, Djokovic had already won a Grand Slam. But he did it by excelling on *defense*. One reason he brought on Martin was to learn how to play a more offense-oriented game, in which he hit the ball as hard in matches as he did during that first hitting session with Todd.

"It's a lot easier to work with Novak Djokovic on these things than it is with Sally or Barney down at the local club,"

Todd said. But the goal is the same: tennis that's equally aggressive and confident in practice and in matches, which is
only possible if you know how hard you're swinging in the
first place. As Martin puts it, "The best players in the world
play with great intention and purpose with regard to pace."

True for them, and for you.

23

Strategy: Plan A

Suppose you want to drive from Chicago to St. Louis. You pull onto the interstate and head south—except there's construction ahead, and since you can't stand sitting in traffic, you get off at the next exit. To the left is a strip mall, and to the right is one of those old-fashioned diners you loved so much when you were a kid. You turn right, so you can drive past the diner. Then you keep going, past office parks, through a charming little town. After a while, you come to a traffic light. The light's red, and you don't feel like waiting, so you do a U-turn and head back the other way, until suddenly, to your left, you see a side street shaded with trees. You turn left and drive through a beautiful neighborhood, past bungalows and colonial homes. A few miles later, the street turns into a state highway, and before you know it, you're breezing through farmland and cornfields as far as the eye can see.

Five hours later, you pull into a truck stop. You ask the clerk where you are, check a map, and discover you're nowhere near St. Louis. You're stymied. *How did this happen?* It's four and a half hours from Chicago to St. Louis, and you've been driving nearly six hours—how come you're not there by now?

You think about it for a few minutes, and then it hits you. *Oh, I know!* you think. *There must be something wrong with my car!*

You would never drive this way in real life. Only a fool would drive around mindlessly and expect to get where he's supposed to go.

Yet, a lot of tennis players do this every time they play a match! Instead of going into the match with a game plan, they simply react to whatever their opponent throws at them. Then, when they lose, they blame poor technique.

I've got news for you: When you lose a match, it's almost never because of poor technique. Poor strategy is typically to blame.

Or maybe you had no strategy at all.

In a moment, I'll introduce the Plan A Strategy you should take with you into every match. It's simple and actionable. It's also necessary: At lower levels of tennis, you can get by on technique alone, but to win at higher levels, fundamentally sound strategy is a must.

Best of all, strategy is simpler to incorporate into your game than new technique. It's also more effective and its impact more immediate.

Plan A Singles Strategy

The Essential Tennis Plan A Singles Strategy is the smartest, simplest, and highest-percentage method one can employ in a tennis match. It's based on three objective concepts:

1. The geometry of the court.
2. The physics of colliding objects.
3. Human biomechanics.

As you get deeper into any given match, you'll improvise off Plan A as you become aware of your opponents' weaknesses and strengths. Until you do, stick with Plan A—it's your blueprint for every match from now until eternity.

Your singles Plan A Strategy is simple. How simple? How about this:

On the baseline, hit crosscourt until you have a darn good reason not to.

That's it. It really is this easy. In fact, I'm willing to bet that if you were to go out right now and play a match in which you hit only crosscourt, you'd play one of the better matches of your career.

Why crosscourt?

There are five reasons you should hit crosscourt:

1. **The net.** The net is three feet high in the center, three and a half feet high at each end. Hitting crosscourt allows you to hit over the lowest part of the net, reducing the chance of a net error.

2. **The Pythagorean Theorem.** Remember it from middle school: $a^2 + b^2 = c^2$? Pythagorean Theorem tells us that although it's 78 feet from baseline to baseline, it's 82½ feet from one corner of the court to the opposite corner. When you hit crosscourt, the court is suddenly 4½ feet longer—a sizable margin of error.

3. **Redirection.** It's easier to hit a ball back in the direction it came from than to redirect it, for two reasons. First, because the timing required to change the direction of a ball is difficult. Second, because you need to account for the fact that when you redirect a ball, the momentum it has wants to carry it wider than you intend. When you receive a crosscourt shot to your forehand (from the left side of the court to the right side, for a righty), the ball's rightward momentum will continue off your racket face. No longer can you simply line up your strings with your target and have the ball go there—you now have to account for the incoming angle of

the ball. This is the reason so many down-the-line shots are missed wide when one changes the ball's direction.

4. **Recovery.** After every shot, you need to recover to the midpoint of your opponent's two best possible returns. When you hit crosscourt from, say, your deuce-court corner, you place your opponent in her own deuce corner of the court, leaving you just a step or two from being perfectly positioned at the midpoint of her two best possible shots: She can either go straight down-the-line or hit an extreme-angle shot through the deuce-court service box. The midpoint for these two possibilities is slightly right of center along the baseline, very close to where you're already standing. If, however, you hit down-the-line, you *hit yourself out of position*—you now need to move across the baseline, past the hash mark, to place yourself at the midpoint of her two best possible returns, which is now on the ad side. Low-level players continually hit themselves out of position, making it all the more likely they'll hit an error on the next ball (not to mention have to run a lot farther).

5. **Timing.** Rarely will tennis players at any level strike the ball at the precise instant they should. Sometimes we're early, but much more often we're late. When you're late on a crosscourt shot, the ball goes to the middle of the court. If, however, you're

late going down-the-line, the ball sails wide, and you lose the point.

Plan A Strategy states that you hit crosscourt until you have a "darn good reason not to."

What qualifies as a "darn good reason"? Here are the top five:

- **To take advantage of opponent positioning.** Your opponent is wildly out of position, leaving two-thirds of the court or more exposed—plenty of open space into which you can hit a winning shot.
- **To capitalize on opponent weakness.** You've detected a major flaw in your opponent's game—so noticeable that it behooves you to hit down-the-line to his weak side.
- **To utilize your best asset.** Your down-the-line forehand or backhand is your best shot—one you've honed and can hit consistently.
- **To change the pattern.** If exchanging crosscourt shots on the deuce side gives you much less chance of winning the point than exchanging crosscourt shots on the ad side, then a calm, high-margin down-the-line shot to change the directional pattern might be a good idea.
- **To approach the net.** The geometry of the court completely changes when you're up at the net. An

ideal recovery position is on the same side of the court as the shot you just hit (instead of being crosscourt, when you're on the baseline). That means hitting your approach shot down-the-line minimizes how much you need to run and maximizes your chances of intercepting your opponent's next shot.

Singles

What about hitting volleys in singles—what's your strategy then?

Once again, it's simple. But this time, it depends on your level of control in the point.

1. **Defensive or neutral position.** When you're off balance or challenged at the net—what we call a defensive situation—keep the ball in front of you, in order not to expose a wide-open court for your opponent. When you're in a neutral situation (neither player has a clear advantage), then you can hit down-the-line or crosscourt, but remember that crosscourt means much more movement to cover the next shot!
2. **Offensive position.** When you're balanced and in control of the point, put the ball away by using a crosscourt shot or sharp angle.

Doubles

You might think that with four players on the court, the Plan A Strategy would get more complicated. In fact, it's simpler:

Keep the ball away from the opponent who's closest to you, until you have a clear opportunity to attack.

This applies whether you're playing at the baseline or the net.

When I teach strategy to students, one of the first things they'll often ask me is, "What if my opponent figures out that all I'm doing is hitting crosscourt?"

My reply is always the same: "Who cares?"

Tennis isn't Battleship—you don't win by tricking your opponent or keeping your strategy secret. Nor is it poker—you can't bluff your way to a win. Tennis is a game of execution: The player who executes an effective strategy best while making the fewest mistakes is the one who wins, every single time. It doesn't matter if your opponent or anyone else knows how you're doing it.

A real-world example of this is the rivalry between Federer and Nadal. When Roger and Rafa play each other, every sportswriter, TV commentator, and knowledgeable fan in the stadium knows Rafa's plan—and so does Roger. Rafa's main tactic against Federer (and pretty much every opponent) is to hit high to the backhand until there's enough open court to pound a forehand winner. Nadal's strategy is to bet his forehand against every backhand in the world. He knows he'll lose plenty of points along the way. He also knows that so long as he wins more than half of them, he wins.

Federer and his team are 100 percent aware of Nadal's plan, but it doesn't matter. Nadal has the better head-to-head record because on average he has executed his plan more consistently and effectively than Roger has been able to adjust.

This Plan A Strategy is effective only to the extent that you use it. It's common for players to try it but then quickly go back to whatever they typically do (usually just reacting to whatever their opponent hits them). This might happen because they get bored with it or don't find it fun. Or they believe that, intelligent as it may be, they're good enough to deviate from it.

What they don't realize is that players far better than they are sticking to the Plan A Strategy like it's the Bible. Hitting crosscourt isn't some entry-level strategy that you graduate from once you're good enough. Quite the contrary: It's the tactic many professional players use as the foundation of their game.

TAKE ACTION

Progression 1

Watch one set of a professional match. Notice how often the players hit crosscourt. When they *do* deviate from hitting crosscourt, what were the circumstances, and what happened? Do more errors occur when they hit crosscourt or when they deviate from the Plan A Strategy?

Progression 2

Film yourself playing a set or tiebreak. Play your normal style, with no attempt to use Plan A. Watch the footage and take note of how often you do and don't hit crosscourt. What's the balance? How do points typically end for you when you deviate from Plan A?

Progression 3

Play an entire match in which you hit *only* crosscourt—even if you have a good reason not to. What's the result? Did you ever have the urge to hit down-the-line only to realize, in hindsight, that it's better you didn't?

24

Warm Up Like
Sherlock Holmes

Tennis is the only major sport in the world in which the opponents actually help each other get warmed up.

It doesn't happen in baseball—you'll never see the Red Sox throw batting practice to the Yankees. Foreman never helped Ali stretch his quads. Not once did Jordan feed bounce passes to Bird before a game so Larry could practice his jump shot.

But tennis players? We're a friendly bunch. So friendly that we voluntarily engage in a five-minute cooperative rally before every match, the sole purpose of which is to help each other get loose.

It's beautiful when you think about it—a shining example of reciprocity, sportsmanship, and mutual respect.

Or is it?

If I were to ask you what the purpose of the pre-match warm-up was, you'd probably say, "Duh! To warm up!"

But that'd be only half right.

Actually, less than half. If I had to quantify it, I'd say that grooving your strokes, getting the blood flowing, and loosening up is 20 percent of the reason you do a pre-match warm-up.

Why only 20 percent? Because if you're serious about winning, you will have already done a fifteen- to thirty-minute warm-up on your own, complete with dynamic stretches, practice serves, and hitting at the wall. (See chapter 29 for more on that.)

And the other 80 percent?

Intel—i.e., gathering intelligence on your opponent.

The primary goal of the pre-match hit-around is to figure out your opponent's weaknesses and strengths, so you can begin putting together a game plan before the match even starts.

In other words, the purpose of the warm-up isn't self-assessment—it's *other-guy* assessment. As you hit with your opponent, the question you should ask yourself isn't "How am I feeling today?" but "How is *he* feeling today?"

This goes back to an idea I introduced in chapter 2—that tennis is a game of errors and your job is to do things that cause your opponent to make them. It's also based on the notion that it's much easier to make your opponent play poorly than to make yourself play fantastically.

Of course, the only way you can make opponents play poorly is if you're aware of their weaknesses and the holes in their game. Based on what you find out, you put together a game plan—one that complements the Plan A Strategy I introduced in the previous chapter. And then, of course, you need to implement that game plan and pound away at your opponents' weaknesses, over and over, until they cause him to crumble.

What sort of intelligence should you be looking for during the hit-around, and what's the best way to find it out?

Here are the specific things you should do in every warm-up:

1. **Test your opponent's forehand and backhand.** Hit a few shots to both his forehand and backhand. Is one noticeably weaker than the other?

2. **Take him left and right.** Move him left and right, too—nothing excessive, because this is, after all, a cooperative rally in which neither player tries to dominate the other. But a player should do enough to see if his opponent can (or can't) remain on balance and hit cleanly on the move.

3. **Hit directly at him.** I'll go ahead and steal this one from coach/former player/TV commentator/au-

thor Brad Gilbert. In *Winning Ugly*, Brad suggests you hit three shots directly at your opponent—then pay attention to which type of shot he chooses to hit. Does he run around each one and make it a forehand? Or a backhand? If he consistently chooses one, that means the other one is likely his weaker shot—and the one you will proceed to hit to over and over throughout the match.

4. **Go high and loopy.** Hit a few deep balls with lots of arc. Your opponent will do one of three things:

   - **Stand his ground and take the ball at shoulder height or higher.** Even if he succeeds in getting the ball back, this is a difficult shot that will lead to either an error or a weak return. If this is how he responds, continue to hit high and deep during the match—and be prepared to move in and attack.

   - **Step back and allow the ball to drop.** This is a neutral response. He won't necessarily suffer from high, loopy balls, but do take note of where his returns land. Often, they'll be short—an invitation for you to move forward and close out the point.

   - **Move forward and take the ball on the rise.** If he does this and remains on balance without giving up errors or weak replies, tip your cap and don't give him more high-and-loopy shots.

5. **Hit short and bring him in.** Players put a lot of effort

into running their opponents back and forth across the court. But it can be more effective to move them forward and back. Most singles players aren't great at transitioning forward to the net. So test him out: When you hit short (deliver a shot that lands inside his service box), does your opponent come forward and field it comfortably? Does he recognize it late and lunge? Or does he—heaven help him!—*allow the ball to bounce twice*? If he does either of the last two, plan to bring him forward all day. He either doesn't know how to do it, doesn't like to, or, very likely, both.

6. **Employ backspin.** A good slice will stay low after the bounce and either skid or check up, requiring your opponent to supply all the power. Is he able to return your slice with a mix of power and spin? Or does he net the ball, or send a line drive into the back fence?

7. **Observe volleys.** When your opponent takes his turn at the net, the first thing you should notice is where he stands. A good volleyer will begin fielding deep volleys and half volleys around the service line and slowly transition forward. If, however, your opponent positions himself about a racket's length from the net or less, he's way too close—an indication that he isn't comfortable playing net and would prefer to stay back.

Next, take note of whether he volleys equally well on both the forehand and backhand sides. Most players have a preference.

Hit some low ones, too. How does he react when the contact point is below the top of the net? Is he calm and relaxed, softening his grip to avoid the net while keeping his return deep? Or does he reflexively tighten up and lose control?

Finally, hit a few shots directly at his chest, but not hard—that would be unsportsmanlike, and something I'd never advocate. Try to see if he can handle this challenging shot. If he panics, it means he's not super comfortable at the net and would likely rather stay back.

By the way—I said that the first thing you should notice is where your opponent stands when it's his turn to volley. That's actually the second thing. The first is whether he bothers to volley at all. Some players don't—a clear signal they don't know how and never will, unless you force them to. Which you will.

8. **Watch overheads.** When you hit your opponent an overhead, pay attention to where his smash lands. If his smashes land in the net or way out, keep hitting him lots of overheads during the match. Likewise, if his smashes go anywhere but back to you, it means he likely can't control where they go and would rather not receive them.

As with volleys, not all players will request overheads. If they don't, or if they refuse when you offer, *BINGO!*—overhead time!

9. **Your serve: Find the 1 of 4.** If you're able to place your serves, hit a few to each of the four corners: wide and down-the-T in each service box. Watch how your opponent returns them. Of these four targets, one will be your opponent's weakest and one his strongest. Also notice how he responds to drive, slice, and kick, including his overall swing confidence, movement, and balance.

10. **Be alert to technique "prettiness."** In general, are all of your opponent's strokes equally smooth, balanced, and "pretty"? Or does one (or more) stand out as choppy and clearly unrefined? Find your opponent's ugliest stroke and assume this is the one most likely to break down.

11. **Analyze overall psychological states.** They're often overlooked, but extremely important.

    How happy is your opponent to be here? Is he energetic, excited, and glad he's on court? Or is he pouty or whiny, and does he seem like he'd rather be anywhere else?

    When he makes a mistake, does he shake it off and move on, or does he whine and curse himself—"Come on, you idiot!" Do you see any hints of frustration, and if so, are they linked to a particular shot? (He might even say something: "Geez, my backhand!")

    If you detect a low emotional state, your best play is "nothing fancy"—just do your thing and

allow your opponent to self-destruct. But beware:
His negativity could be contagious, so you can't
allow yourself to get sucked into that space.

It goes without saying that throughout all this, you should also take note of opponents' strengths. Do they have a go-to shot that they love to nail and are able to consistently? If yes, avoid setting them up for it.

I realize this is a lot of information, so when you're starting out, keep it simple. You don't need to put together a thirty-page scouting report. One or two actionable takeaways is enough to build a winning game plan.

What if your big takeaway from the warm-up is "Dang! He's good at everything!"

It's certainly possible, particularly at higher levels of play, that no major weakness will stand out. But even on the tour, players are *relatively* worse at some things than others.

So look for that: your opponent's relative weaknesses, or least competent strengths, so at least you can start with something.

TAKE ACTION

Progression 1

Attend a local tennis match as a spectator—perhaps a high school or college match, or a match at your neighborhood courts or club. Watch the players warm up and see if you can detect their weaknesses and strengths. Based on what you see, what tactics would you implement against each player? Watch how the match pans out and see how accurate your predictions were.

Progression 2

When you play a match, warm up like Sherlock Holmes: Be a detective and pick out two actionable takeaways based on how your opponent hits during the pre-match rally. Then choose one of these weaknesses and make it the basis for your strategy, pounding away at this weakness throughout the match.

As you get more comfortable with this, you'll put together an entire game plan based on what you observe in the warm-up. For now, one actionable takeaway is enough.

25

Eye off the Ball

That's a typo, right? Isn't Rule #1 of tennis that you should always, *always* keep your eye on the ball?

Actually, no. From the moment the ball leaves your opponent's racket until you make contact, you most definitely want to keep your eye on the ball. But once the ball leaves your racket, your point of focus is no longer the ball—it's *your opponent*.

This might contradict what coaches have shouted at you for years during your tennis lessons—"Come on, eye on the ball!" But here's the thing: If you watch only the ball, you miss out on valuable information that will help you *anticipate* the shot your opponent is going to hit back to you. Anticipating allows you to move to the right place earlier, set up more correctly and faster, choose the best possible target, and play a less frantic, more relaxed game.

Many people assume that anticipation is a gift—one of those magical talents that you're either born with or you're not. But anticipation is a skill like any other, and can be learned.

Here's how it works:

After you strike the ball, shift your gaze to your opponent. Pay attention to the following clues—I call them the Four Ps:

1. **Preparation**

   How your opponent prepares her racket and body is the biggest determinant of what shot she's about to hit.

   - **Racket face.** If your opponent's racket is open (contact-side strings facing up), she's going to hit a slice, drop shot, lob, or something else *without lots of power.* Why? Because to hit with power, a player needs to hit the ball flat or with topspin— neither of which are possible when the strings face up during preparation.

     If, however, her racket is closed (strings facing down), expect an aggressive incoming shot.

   - **Stance.** When Serena Williams sets up in an open stance, it means . . . nothing. She can drive the ball crosscourt, take it down-the-line, or do pretty much anything else she wants with it. This goes for almost all players at the professional level. Once you start working your way down, however, you find that certain players are more comfortable hitting certain kinds of shots from specific stances. For example, a player might be able to hit to anywhere on the court from a neutral stance, but once he's in an open stance, he can *only* go down-the-line. On the backhand, it's often even more prominent—some players can hit their backhands only to a certain spot. This is something you should pay attention to in the warm-up and first few games of the match. Once you figure it out, you'll immediately know what shot is coming based on how your opponent sets up.

That said, there is one stance-related rule that's true at every level: If at any time your opponent rotates so far that you can see her back, move forward immediately! You're likely about to receive a short ball, which you can then attack.

The one exception, of course, is if you're already at the net. In this case, your opponent will probably try for a high, deep lob over your head. When you're already up, moving closer to the net would make it even easier for your opponent to lob you—so hold tight and see how good of a defensive shot they're able to pull off.

- **Coil.** Is your opponent setting up in a strong,

athletic turn of her upper body with her racket taken back into a loaded position? If so, an aggressive shot is almost certainly on the way.

- If, on the other hand, she's barely turned and the racket is thrust out toward the ball, that indicates that a weak shot will likely be delivered.

2. **Posture**

This refers to the extent that your opponent is or is not in balance.

If your opponent is perfectly balanced—torso evenly split between the legs with a clean axis down the middle, standing mostly upright with a slight bend in the knees—she's poised to deliver power. Get ready for a monster of a shot.

If she's not in balance, here's what you might expect:

If your opponent is at all bent over, shoulders low, look for a short, weak return.

If your opponent has been knocked off her axis in any way, she's in a compromised position and will be unable to hit as aggressively or accurately as she'd like.

Pay attention to how compressed or stretched she is. If she's jammed, making contact too close to the body, her shot will be short and lack power; if she's stretched out, she'll most likely go down-the-line—it's difficult to hit across one's body when fully extended.

3. **Position**

This is your opponent's location on the court and the extent to which she is or isn't in an ideal place to receive the ball. Possibilities include:

- **Emergency.** She's in an all-out sprint and needs to hit on the run. She doesn't have time to set up; her only goal is to somehow get her racket on the ball. Expect a high, slow return down-the-line or toward the middle; from her current position, it would be almost impossible to hit aggressively crosscourt.

- **Pressured.** Not as bad as "emergency," but not comfortable, either. Your opponent has some control over her body and racket but is required to move and receive the ball in a less-than-ideal way. Expect a similar result as above—high and down-the-line or to the middle, with little power. Crosscourt is a possibility, but still difficult to pull off.

- **Challenging rally ball.** Your opponent has to move, but not much. This ball is just outside the realm of "comfort zone" and she can strike the ball without being stretched. Expect crosscourt to be more likely than in the previous situation. The oddsmaker in my head is now considering my opponent's preferences, patterns of play, and special skills.

- **Moving backward.** If your opponent backs up from the baseline, it's an indicator that you're about to receive a short return. Many players don't make up for the court position they've sacrificed—they hit their typical baseline return instead of a high, deep shot to compensate for having moved back.

- **Rally ball.** Not too challenging, not too easy. Expect your opponents to return toward their favorite target.

- **Offensive attack.** At this point, your opponent is in total control and can hit to any target using any type of reply that they're comfortable with. Now the name of the game is pattern recognition. Where have they aimed similar shots so far in this match? Do they have any clear preferences for finishing shots? If so, now is the time to move in that direction. If you're wrong, so be it—but better to commit than to stand flat-footed and get beat in either direction.

4. **Preferences and Patterns of Play**

Each of us has our favorite shots. Your opponent's go-to shot might be an exception that goes against the rule—perhaps an incredible on-the-run forehand down-the-line or a closed-stance backhand crosscourt. The good news is, if your opponent does have a trick up her sleeve, you'll most likely find out early. As soon as you see it, take note— she's probably going to hit the same shot again in similar situations later on. If it's a consistently fantastic shot, your best play would be to avoid giving her an opportunity to hit it again.

TAKE ACTION

If you've never tried to anticipate your opponent's shots, you might feel overwhelmed—the idea of watching her racket, shoulders, posture, and how she moves, while also keeping in mind her unique skills and favorite shots, and then synthesizing this in a span of one or two seconds so that you can take action and *move* . . . sounds impossible.

But trust me, you'll get better at it. For now, start slowly, one P at a time.

Progression 1

Go to your local courts or attend a tournament as a spectator, and watch a match. Choose one player and see if you can predict what his next shot will be, based on just one of the Four Ps. After a while, switch to the other player and do the same thing.

Then do the whole thing again with a different P. Eventually try two, three, or all four Ps together.

This is an ideal way to start, because you're not involved in the action, so you can put 100 percent of your focus on the clues that will help you anticipate.

Progression 2

The next time you practice, focus on one of the Four Ps and see if you can anticipate your partner's shots. Forget about your own technique entirely—all mental energy should go into anticipating.

Progression 3

Hit with a partner and try to incorporate two, three, or even all four Ps to anticipate what's coming next.

Progression 4

The first time you try to anticipate in a match, work with only one of the Four Ps. Your desire to win will make it too difficult to use them all.

As you get better, keep adding Ps until you're comfortable using all four.

26

(Not Necessarily) Better to Serve Than to Receive

Every tennis match starts with a coin toss, racket spin, or rock-scissors-paper to figure out who serves first and who starts on which side.

If you win the toss, what should you choose?

It depends on your answer to two questions:

Question one: How big is your serve?

Question two: How big is your ego?

. . .

A lot of players don't realize it, but whoever wins the pre-match toss has three options: serve or receive; side of the court; or defer, and let the other player choose.

Many players assume that the correct choice is "serve." They might not necessarily want to, but they're afraid of looking weak, coming across as unconfident, or sending the wrong message ("I'm not a formidable competitor!") if they don't choose to serve.

For about 20 percent of the tennis-playing population, serving first *is* the right choice. For everyone else, the smarter move is to put ego aside and choose "receive."

Here's why:

Deciding whether to serve or receive, pick a certain side, or defer to your opponent comes down to one thing: What will give you an immediate advantage, straight out of the gate?

If your serve is a weapon and you can consistently get it in, then by all means, *serve*! But what I've found is that at beginning and intermediate levels of tennis (3.5 and below), the serve is not yet a reliable weapon. At best, it's a neutral event to get the point started, akin to rolling the dice when you play Monopoly; at worst, the serve is detrimental. Players at 3.0 and below often have trouble getting their serve in at all. And when they do, they feed their opponents the one shot they're typically most comfortable with—the ground stroke of their choice.

Around 4.0 (the advanced-intermediate level), players start purposefully using their serve in a way that challenges opponents. But only at 4.5 and above—the top 10 percent of players in the world—is the server able to use power, spin, and placement in a way that makes his serve a true weapon.

At or below 3.5, the best way to put yourself at an immediate advantage is to *make your opponent serve*. Put the pressure on him. Force him to get his serves in at the start of the match, when he's still not fully warmed up.

Meanwhile, even if you're 4.0 or above, I suggest you receive, unless all three of the following conditions apply:

1. **Your serve is a weapon.** You hit lots of aces, or opponents consistently struggle to return your first serve, and sometimes your second serve as well.

2. **You've had a chance to fully warm up your serve.** I'm not talking about the token five or six serves players take before a match. I mean, you got to the court early, did dynamic stretches for fifteen minutes, and hit at least twenty serves from each side—a healthy mix of flat, kick, and slice—to the point where you're certain your serve is ready.

3. **You're "on."** You feel great, your timing's good, and you're confident about the match before it starts.

If any of these conditions does not apply, choose to receive—and put the pressure on your opponent.

That said, even if all three conditions are in place, you might choose to receive if you're a slow starter. Some players need a few games, or even an entire set, to get comfortable. If this describes you, give yourself an extra game to get acclimated.

What about the sun—should it be a factor?

In singles, sunshine matters less, because both players will eventually serve into the sun. But if your opponent wins the toss and elects to serve, pick the side of the court that puts the sun in your opponent's eyes to start.

In doubles, meanwhile, once a player serves on a particular side, she'll continue to serve on that side for the duration of the set. This means that if you and your partner are a lefty-righty combo, you can go the entire match without either of you having to serve into the sun—so think carefully when deciding who serves where and when.

Another option is to "defer" to your opponent and let him choose. The only good reason I can think of for doing this would be to mess with your opponent's head. I don't recommend it.

If, however, your opponent wins the toss and defers to you or chooses "side," make him serve, for this reason: If he felt good about his serve, he would have chosen it. Why not make him do something he didn't choose to do?

REFLECT

Serve-Receive Awareness

In your journal, keep track of whether you serve or receive first in your next ten matches. Is there a relationship between which one you do first and the outcome of the match? How about the outcome of the first set? In which situation do you feel more comfortable, relaxed, and able to play your best tennis for the entire match?

27

Serves II:
First and Second

Most amateur tennis players want to overpower their opponent on their first serve, and on the second to "just get it in."

Neither part of this approach is completely correct. To understand why, you need to understand the difference between
first and second serves, including the purpose and methodol-
ogy behind each.

First Serve: "Hard" vs. "Hard for them"

The common assumption is that first serves are all about
power. And while they *may* be, they don't have to be. I prefer
to think of the first serve as whichever serve gives you

the best chance to beat the opponent you're playing that particular day. It's not necessarily about hitting your serve hard, but about hitting what's hard for your opponent to return.

During the pre-match warm-up and first few games, pay attention to how opponents handle each of your serves. If they struggle with your kick and slice, you should continue to hit these spin serves as a first serve, even if they're not necessarily your most powerful.

This was the exact approach I took when I played in college. Whether I was playing singles or doubles, I rarely hit flat, powerful first serves. I relied much more on my slice. As a lefty, my slice sails into the body of right-handed opponents when I aim for their dominant side, a more effective play than trying to overpower them with something flat that stays on the same horizontal plane.

In addition to your opponent's weaknesses, you should take into account how your various serves are "feeling" that day. If for whatever reason your awesome 130-mph flat serve won't stay in the box, it doesn't matter how lethal it is. So ditch it for whatever's working.

Second Serve: "The strings send, the path bends."

To make sure they don't double-fault, many players decelerate the racket head on their second serve, thinking that if they swing *very carefully* they'll avoid making a mistake.

In fact, it's the opposite: On a second serve, you should swing as aggressively as you can control—just as aggressively as you do on a flat, powerful first serve. The only difference is the path of your swing:

> On a first serve, you swing up at the ball and follow through in the direction of your target; on a second serve, you swing up and out to the side, away from your target.

Why "up and out"? Because the up-and-out swing path gives you the two things you need to guarantee the serve goes in: ample net clearance and massive spin, which dips the ball back down into the box. The harder you swing, the more of each you get; decelerating, on the other hand, diminishes each, and increases the chance of a double fault.

When working with students, I tell them to think of the second-serve swing path as a rainbow over the baseline. As long as the strings face the service box when you make contact, that's where the ball's going to go. The path of the racket—up and out—is what leads to the arc, or bend, in the serve as it curves up and over the net, then down into the court. Hence one of my favorite teaching expressions: "The strings send, the path bends."

The paradox here is that when you find yourself in a pressure situation—say, up 40–30 in a pivotal game, or down match point—and you absolutely *must* get your second serve in, you're going to *want* to swing slower in an effort to exert control—but don't! Overcome your fear instinct and swing as aggressively as you would if you were up five games to none, 40-love. Be sure to swing up and out, along the baseline, so you get the safety you need to keep the serve in.

In addition to providing a comfortable margin for error, the up-and-out swing path does something else—it causes the ball to "kick" up and into the face of your opponent after the bounce (hence the term "kick serve"). Almost no one enjoys returning a strong kick serve. One of the most difficult things to do in tennis is strike a ball that's still rising up at you as you swing. The most your opponent will likely be able to do is hit a weak return to mid-court, allowing you to dictate the rest of the point.

For this reason, many pro players often use a kick serve as a first serve, Dominic Thiem being one of them. One of the quickest ways to take your game to the next level is to develop an aggressive kick serve you can use in any situation.

DRILL: SEND AND BEND

If you're not familiar with how to hit a second serve, start with these progressions:

Progression 1

Address the baseline in your normal service stance. Take a ball in your tossing hand and put it up above your head, out in front of you. Now sandwich the ball between your tossing hand and your racket face so your racket is aligned horizontally (parallel to the court surface). Roll the ball up and down the palm of your tossing hand with your racket face to get a feel for what vertical movement at contact is like.

Progression 2

After a minute or two of rolling the ball up and down the palm of your hand, accelerate your racket up past the fingertips of your tossing hand and trace a "rainbow" path with the tip of your racket as it continues upward, along the baseline, and then out to the right (if you're right-handed). The ball should roll up off your fingertips and slightly forward past your hand. Before you get to the end of the "rainbow" out to your right, make sure your hand turns so the palm of your hand is facing the back fence behind the baseline.

Progression 3

After rolling the ball up off your fingertips and completing a "rainbow" with your hand facing the back fence, complete a follow-through by tracing the racket back along the baseline and across the front of your body to the left (for a righty).

Progression 4

After several minutes getting familiar with the rolls, rain-
bows, and finishes, try tossing a ball and completing the exact
same swing path and finish. Listen for an aggressive "clicking" or "brushing" noise at contact. That's the sound of lots of
spin!

TAKE ACTION

Once you're familiar with the up-and-out swing path, try this:
Play an entire set in which you and your opponent are each
allowed only one serve. This will help you practice hitting
serves that are both aggressive and go in.

28

Return-of-Serve I:
Serve + 1

Quiz time!

1. Which of these rally lengths is the most common in
   a professional tennis singles point, counting the
   serve as one shot?
   a. 0–1 shots
   b. 2–3
   c. 4–8
   d. 9+
2. What is the most common rally length in an amateur 4.0-level adult tennis point?

a. 0–1 shots

b. 2–3

c. 4–8

d. 9+

3. In the past six months, how many times have you consciously set aside time to practice your serve?

a. 0–1

b. 2–3

c. 4–8

d. 9+

4. During that period of time, how many times did you practice your return-of-serve?

a. 0–1

b. 2–3

c. 4–8

d. 9+

Before I reveal the answers, I should warn you: You might not like what you're about to hear.

Why?

Because it will change how you think about how you allocate your time on court and what it means to practice, in a way that could make practicing seem less fun. It might also cause you to regret having wasted so much time practicing shots you rarely need to hit when you should have been drilling the two that you need most—and that are most likely to help you win.

. . .

Every so often, I come across a statistic that blows my mind. I was shocked to learn that even the most dominant players in the world win only slightly more than 50 percent of their points, and lose almost half. (We talked about that in chapter 1.)

This next set of statistics comes to us from the same source—coach, consultant, and the founder of Brain Game Tennis, Craig O'Shannessy.

After exhaustive research, Craig found that most professional tennis points end with a double fault (0 shots) or an ace or unreturned serve (1 shot). So the answer to the first question in the quiz is "a": 2.5 percent of points end with a double fault, and 29.5 percent end with a serve that isn't returned.

Craig then studied matches at the 4.0 level. You might think that an amateur tennis point would last longer, since the ball travels so much slower than in the pros and players have more time to track the ball, set up, and execute. But once again, the answer is "a": 12 percent end with a double fault, and 26 percent end with either an ace or the returner hitting for an error.

Based on his observations, Craig is fairly sure that the same holds true at every level of the game. Whether we're talking about the most rudimentary level of tennis or the most advanced, the most common rally length is *one shot or less*.

Allow that to sink in for a moment. Think about all the time you've spent working on your forehand—the lessons, hitting sessions with teammates and friends, shadow swings in the garage, hours watching instructional videos on You-Tube and footage of pros so you can figure out how to make your forehand like theirs . . . And yet a third of the time, you'll never need to hit it because the return-of-serve never makes it into play.

Which leads us to questions 3 and 4:

Based on my experience coaching committed adult students, my sense is that most serious players practice their serve at least once a month, usually more. Very few, however—as in, almost none—practice their return-of-serve, *ever*—even though it's the one shot that, along with the serve, they are guaranteed to be required to hit on about 50 percent of all points in any given match.

To put it differently: The return-of-serve is the least practiced, yet most important, shot in tennis. Here's why players don't practice it:

1. **It's impractical.** The return-of-serve is the one shot you can't practice alone. Ball machines, walls, and self-feeds just aren't the same; to properly practice your return, you need a live practice partner who's willing to hit serve after serve while you return.

2. **It's not fun.** Fact 1: Most players aren't great at returning serve. Fact 2: Most players would rather practice the shots they're already good at and avoid the ones they're not. (If you don't believe me, go ahead and think back on your own practice regimen and how much time you spend practicing what.) Result: Players don't practice returning serve because they don't want to.

3. **They assume it's just like a regular ground stroke.** It's not! Returning serve is an entirely different animal, requiring its own unique set of skills.

4. **They think it's not important.** Players consider the return-of-serve as a mere formality—the way you get things started before the *real* point begins. But about one third of the time the serve and return-of-serve *is* the point.

In the next chapter, I'll show you how to practice the second-most-important shot in tennis—the return.

But first, some final thoughts on these incredible stats.

Craig's findings are revolutionizing the way high-level players train. For years, players practiced hitting, hitting, and more hitting until they could attain a robot-like consistency on their strokes.

Now, however, coaches are waking up to the idea that all this rallying back and forth doesn't matter as much as they thought. Because what *really* wins tennis matches is the ability to hit a great serve or return, followed by one more shot—a concept called Serve + 1 and Return + 1. These days, high-level practices spend more time developing skills and strategy related to Serve/Return + 1 and less to endless ground strokes.

If you want to win more matches, you need to do the same: Instead of "hitting," you might spend 30 percent of your time working on your serve, 30 percent on your return, and the rest on ground strokes, overheads, and volleys.

I realize this might not be as fun as hitting. But you know what's even more fun than hitting? Winning. And to win, you have to master your serve and return.

29

Return-of-Serve II: The X Factor

Time for a confession:

In the last chapter, I said that the serve is the most important shot in tennis, because it's the only shot over which you have complete control. The first half of this statement is true—the serve *is* the most important shot in tennis. But the second part, about "complete control"? As it turns out, it isn't true. At least, not all the time. Here's why:

When a server steps to the baseline and sees a world-class returner-of-serve staring back at him—a Novak Djokovic, a Serena Williams, or the one I and many others consider the best of all time, an Andre Agassi—that server is likely to panic. He knows that no matter how good his serve is, that top-notch returner is likely going to get it back—and maybe even strike it for a winner. At that point, the server is no longer in complete control of his serve—the returner has wrested some of that control away.

My goal for this chapter is to turn you into a one-of-a-kind returner the likes of Agassi et al., so that you, too, will elicit fear in your opponents as they step up to the baseline to serve.

I want to clear up a big misconception about the return-of-serve—specifically, what a good return looks like. There's this notion out there that a good return-of-serve is a screaming line drive that rockets past your opponent for a winner, while he stands frozen in his tracks, mouth agape.

This *would* be an incredible return. It is not, however, the only kind of incredible return. What qualifies as a lethal return-of-serve depends on the type of serve that was hit and how well the typical player might be expected to respond.

In other words, the definition of "awesome return" is fluid. You might think of it as a ladder:

Level 1: Get it back. If your opponent is a huge server (think John Isner), simply getting the ball back, over the net and in, counts as an incredible return.

Level 2: Return with depth and power. The next rung up the ladder is a return in which you get the ball back deep and with pace. Against the majority of quality serves, this is as good as it gets—so congratulate yourself when you accomplish it.

Level 3: Return hard for a winner. At the top of the ladder is the return we all dream about: a powerful shot hit to a specific target for a winner. These are the returns that make the highlight reel.

In my estimation, amateur players put too much emphasis on this third type of return—the rocket-like winner. The truth is, these highlight-reel returns almost never happen. For this reason, I suggest you focus on the first two kinds of returns. They're easier to learn how to execute. They're also the returns that, statistically, will most help you win. Since the most common rally length is one shot or less, if you can just get the ball back, you've already significantly increased your chances of winning the point, and all the more so if you can return the ball with depth and power.

Level 1 and 2 returns are also what made Agassi the phenomenal returner he was. He hit plenty of line-drive winners in his time, but what made Agassi outstanding was his ability to return challenging serves that other players would have missed outright—and, in doing so, keeping himself in the point.

To become an Agassi-like returner, you need to master three things: the Science, the Art, and the X Factor of returning serve:

Technical Skills: The Science

To be a strong returner, you need to be able to *take the ball early*—"on the rise," as we coaches say. This means striking the ball while it's still on its way up from the bounce. Taking the ball early requires three technical skills: lightning-quick reaction time, abbreviated racket takeback, and clean contact in the middle of the strings.

Shot Selection: The Art

One of Agassi's many talents was that he always seemed to know which type of return to hit. On any given serve, you have three choices and less than half a second to decide:

a. **Defensive Return:** In an emergency, Agassi simply got his racket on the ball and put it in play. He did this by switching to a Continental grip and using almost no backswing.

b. **Neutral Return:** If the incoming serve was powerful, but not so much that it was an emergency, then Andre would drive the ball confidently with purpose and try to set up each point in a favorable way.

c. **Offensive Return:** Once in a while, Agassi received a serve that he could wallop for an aggressive return—and when he did, he knew it almost immediately.

Anticipation: The X Factor

The only way Agassi could do any of these things was by *anticipating* what serve was coming and where it was headed.

I call anticipation the "X Factor," because this ability makes the all-time greats stand out. It's mysterious—unlike technical skills and shot selection, anticipation is a seeming sixth sense about the serve you're about to receive.

That said, anticipation can be learned, like any skill. I happen to think anticipation is the easiest of the serve skills to develop, because all you have to do is *observe*—and then not be afraid to move.

To anticipate what serve your opponent is about to hit and where it's headed, you need to:

a. **Read the toss.** If your opponent tosses over his head or behind him, expect a kick serve. A toss directly over his hitting shoulder or slightly outside it indicates a flat serve or moderate slice. A toss far outside the hitting shoulder, meanwhile, signals a heavy slice.

b. **Pick up on patterns.** All players have a go-to serve that they like to hit in certain situations, particularly when under pressure. By the third or fourth game of the match you should know what your opponent's go-to serve is.

c. **Note an opponent's position on the baseline.** The farther away from the center of the baseline your opponent stands, the more angle he's probably trying to create and the more out wide the serve will likely be.

Once you have a sense of what's coming, you need to do the most important step of all:

d. **Take action.** Good anticipators don't just stand

there, they do something. This doesn't mean you should start running to a certain spot before your opponent makes contact; it's more about having a clear picture in your mind of what's probably going to happen and being prepared to explode in that direction. Once in a while, you might decide to dance around an incoming backhand and make it a forehand; Federer in particular loves to do this.

If you move early, is there a chance you'll be wrong? Absolutely! Agassi got burned plenty of times. But in the long run, anticipating pays off. When it does, the reward is double—not only are you positioned for a strong return, but you've also gotten inside your opponent's head with your seeming ability to read his mind.

DRILL: Almost Agassi

Remember, when your opponent is serving, the return is your first chance to make a shot—so your priority is to *get the ball in*! I tell my students that failing to return a serve is the equivalent of a double fault—that's how important the return is.

Once you're able to consistently get the ball back, you're ready to take your game to the next level by working on the Science, Art, and X Factor of the return-of-serve.

GOAL: Master the three elements that make for a world-class returner-of-serve—technical skills, shot selection, and anticipation.

WHERE AND WHAT: On court. You'll need a bucket of balls and a coach or partner.

HOW: 1. Technical Skill: Reaction Time and Takeback: Your partner stands on his service line (not the baseline) and hits medium-paced serves. React quickly—try to pounce on the ball and take it early with a short, compact backswing. Aim for clean, middle-of-the-racket contact.

1. **Shot Selection:** This drill has four rounds. For each, your partner serves from his service line, like above.

   Round 1: Your partner hits twenty serves at a fast pace. Your goal is to get a racket on the ball and put the ball in play, anywhere.

   Round 2: Your partner hits twenty serves at a medium pace. Try to return with power and depth.

   Round 3: This time, you receive twenty serves at a medium-slow pace. Since you have more time, attempt to return to a specific target on the court for a solid shot, either as a line drive or with topspin.

   Round 4: In the final round, your partner serves twenty balls, mixing them up between slow, medium, and fast-paced, so you don't know what's coming. As quickly as you can, decide which return to make—offensive, defensive, or neutral.

2. **Anticipation:** To practice anticipating, have your partner serve from no-man's-land, halfway between his service line and the baseline. He should serve thirty balls in a random mix of flat, kick, and slice, all at a medium pace. Try to anticipate what's coming by reading the toss—then prime yourself to explode in that direction.

VARIATIONS: As you get better, your partner can increase the pace of the incoming serves.

30

The Do-Nothing Volley

My least favorite word in tennis is "punch."

For as long as there's been tennis instruction, coaches have told players to "punch" their volleys. "Punch" implies an active, forceful collision. But here's the thing: Many volleys are what we call a "touch" shot—they require the player to *absorb* the energy of the incoming ball instead of adding to it.

This is why "punch" is a damaging word—it causes you to do the opposite of what you're supposed to in many situations. If you squeeze the grip, thrust your arm forward toward the ball, and remain firm at contact, you lose any ability to absorb energy from an incoming shot. The "touch," or "feel" you need to execute a good volley is gone.

If that's the case, why is "Punch your volley!" still taught? Punching the volley *does* work for one type of volley—a slow, shoulder-high floater that you can aggressively put away for a winner. As it happens, this ball is the easiest to teach, explain, and feed to a student at the net—so it's therefore the one that coaches most often hit to their students when teaching volleys. Students learn "punch," the phrase gains momentum in the coaching vernacular, and players get stuck with a volley that will work in one out of a hundred possible volley situations.

For every different height, depth, and speed of an incoming ball that you receive at the net, there's a different and corresponding amount of firmness or looseness you need to have in your hand in order to produce the perfect response. How firmly or loosely you grip the racket determines the placement and pace of the volley you send back. That's why you can't simply "punch" the ball every time and have good results—each volley requires its own unique combination of firmness vs. looseness of grip.

How firmly you grip the racket, however, will only be effective if you make clean contact with the ball. This is the element of volleying that most players and coaches overlook. They go straight to "punch" without bothering to talk about the most important thing when volleying—that you make contact in the exact center of the racket.

Clean contact is essential, because if you're off by two or three strings, you can no longer effectively absorb the right amount of energy from the incoming ball. The ball will die off the racket and fall well short of where you wanted it to land. That's why when I teach students to volley, my first goal is to make them aware of the two essentials we discussed— clean contact and firmness of grip. Here's how it works:

1. I tell my student to stand a few feet back from the net, turned to the side, her racket up and slightly in front of her.

2. I feed her ball after ball. My only instruction is that she receive each ball in the exact center of the racket. No swing, no step, no weight transfer, and no "punch." Just clean, passive contact. As she does this, I encourage her to experiment with different degrees of firmness in her grip.

I call this exercise the "Do-Nothing Volley," because it requires students to do nothing—no bending, no takeback, no follow-through. For the first time in their tennis lives, students feel what it's like to *absorb* the power of an incoming shot, instead of adding to it. They also discover that they can control the pace and placement of the volley, simply by changing the firmness of their grip. No punch or swing is required, and believe it or not, the ball will still go over the net if it's hit cleanly!

If we have enough time, the student and I will then do variations of this progression. I'll ask the student to purposely receive ten balls in a row off the edge of her racket frame at 12:00 on the racket face. Then, ten balls at 6:00, ten off the frame at 3:00, and ten off the frame at 9:00.

Why do I purposely ask her to hit "framers"? Because it forces the student to concentrate on the exact spot on the racket that's contacting the ball—something players typically don't think about when they volley (or, quite honestly, don't *ever* think about).

Even when I instruct students to make clean contact, vary the firmness of their grip, but otherwise do nothing, ninety-nine out of a hundred students *still* do active stuff! They don't *think* they're doing it . . . but when we watch slow-motion video, it becomes clear they are. They push their arms forward, bend their wrists forward or back, rotate the racket frame, and do plenty of other active movements that exert force on the ball. The "punch" mentality is so ingrained that they simply can't help it.

It's yet another example of why video is so important, particularly with a controlled, nuanced shot like the volley, where any extraneous movement will destroy your chances of making a clean shot.

DRILL: The Do-Nothing Volley

Eventually, you'll learn how to guide your volleys to specific targets on the court. For now, I want you to focus *only* on clean contact and your grip pressure. If you can master that, everything else about volleying will be significantly easier.

As always, I strongly suggest you film yourself when doing progressions. Like my students, you'll probably want to swat or punch at the incoming ball—it's wired into you. Only slow-motion video will tell you if you're truly doing nothing like you should be.

For these progressions, you'll need a ball machine, or a coach or partner.

GOAL: To teach you how to absorb the power of an incoming shot, make clean contact, and change the pace and depth of your volleys by varying the firmness of your grip.

WHERE AND WHAT: On court, with a ball machine, coach, or partner. If necessary, the drill can be done at a hitting wall.

HOW: Set your ball machine to "low," or have your partner hand-feed balls at a slow pace.

Stand three to five feet back from the net and turn to the side. Line up your racket behind the incoming ball. Allow the ball to gently bounce off the center of the racket.

Vary your grip from shot to shot—see what it feels like to receive a ball with a loose grip, tight grip, and everything in between. Notice how the ball comes off your racquet differently when you change your grip pressure.

Otherwise, do nothing!

Can you feel what it's like to *absorb* the power of the incoming shot, as opposed to adding to it?

WHY THE DRILL WORKS: By isolating this one thing—the firmness and feeling of the ball hitting the strings without any other movements—you can start developing feel! "Touch" or "feel" is often regarded as an innate talent or skill, but you can absolutely learn it by focusing on firmness and quality of contact. Adding good feel to the rest of your skills will dramatically improve your tennis.

VARIATIONS

Similar to above, except this time use an extremely loose grip, and have your partner throw the ball like a dart at the center of your racket. You'll experience an exaggerated feeling of what it's like to absorb power; your racket will also naturally recoil back from the point of contact.

When you try this variation, you might instinctively "fight" contact by tensing up and pushing forward. You need to *consciously not do this,* by keeping your racket still and maintaining a loose grip.

Next, try the exercise with your eyes closed. Your only objectives are to be aware of the tension in your hand and wrist and to keep your hand as loose as possible—nothing else. When the ball hits the racket, you will experience "touch" in its purest form.

31

Lessons:
The Student-Coach
Partnership

What does a great tennis lesson look like?

As with much of tennis, your version of an ideal lesson depends on what you want. If your goal is to get exercise, have fun, take a break from the humdrum of daily life, and get a bit better at what you're already good at, pretty much any lesson structure will suit you fine. If this describes you, I think that's great! My ultimate goal is that each player find his or her own version of happiness on the court, whatever form that takes.

If, however, you want to transform your game and get significantly better than you are now, you and your coach need to construct your lessons and training regimen with precision and care—together. Without a strong student-coach partnership, it will be difficult for you to reach your goals.

Unfortunately, not every coach will have "transformation" in mind while giving you a lesson. Here's a few things to look out for if becoming a completely different tennis player is your goal:

1. **Six Shots in Sixty Minutes.** In a generic tennis lesson, you'll spend five minutes warming up, fifteen minutes on your forehand, fifteen minutes on your backhand, another ten on volleys and overheads, and ten minutes of serves to finish it off. In this lesson, you cover everything, but you don't get a chance to go deep on anything. To truly improve any one stroke, you need to spend a long time on it, maybe even on a small element of that stroke as you overwrite ingrained habits with new ones. When I work with students, we'll often spend three consecutive hours on a single stroke as I attempt to help them build it anew.

2. **Instructional Whac-A-Mole.** In the carnival game Whac-A-Mole, you hold a cushioned hammer and bop mechanical moles on the head as they pop out of the game board in random locations. A bad tennis lesson is like Whac-A-Mole: You jump from one thought to the next, attacking whatever problem arises at any given moment, without any through-line focus

on building a new habit. You may have had a lesson like this: Your teacher shouts, "Bend your knees! Good! Now follow through! Hey, what happened to your contact point? Out in front—you can do it. Don't forget those knees . . ." It goes without saying that it's impossible to improve when focusing on so many things at once.

3. **Quantity over Quality.** If you think, "Great lesson— I hit three hundred balls!" you're measuring output based on volume, not necessarily improvement. Your level of *engagement* is far more important than the number of balls you hit. Hitting and running a lot only reinforces the habits you already have. Instead, you need to perform carefully chosen progressions in the correct order under controlled circumstances. My students and I will sometimes work together for forty-five minutes without hitting a single ball. We'll talk about essential principles, do shadow swings and fake tosses, look at video, discuss cause and effect . . . and only then introduce a ball. If you don't take the time to make sure the quality of movement is high before hitting, you'll revert back to your old habits and remain stuck.

4. **No Homework.** As a kid, you probably didn't want to get homework. As a tennis student, you should crave it. Homework needn't be complicated—

shadow swings, footwork patterns, and serve tosses can all be practiced in your living room. You should write down your homework and make sure you and your coach understand the expectations. You should also film yourself, so you can be certain you're performing each progression correctly. It's what you do outside your lesson that will transform your game. No coach can magically make you better in one hour a week.

5. **No Video.** If you want to exercise and have fun, video will interfere. But if you want to change habits, video is a must. I don't care how experienced your coach is, if you don't use video, she's only *guessing* at what a given problem might be. It might be a very well-educated guess, but still a guess. I don't give any input to my students without looking at video first. As I mentioned earlier in this book, contact between ball and strings lasts four milliseconds; so much is happening before, during, and after those four-thousandths of a second that it's sometimes impossible to separate cause from effect, or to know whether a student is progressing in the right direction, without seeing confirmation in slow-motion video.

6. **One-Size-Fits-All.** After your next lesson, stick around the courts and watch twenty minutes of the lesson that follows yours. If it's the same content as

you received, explained in the same way, you need to speak to your coach about putting together a lesson plan that suits your specific goals, needs, and athletic history.

7. **Buzzwords.** Not all buzzwords are bad, but over the years, coaches have come to rely on certain catchphrases that are either unhelpful, wrong, or both. Even when these phrases are valid, players have heard them so many times that they're desensitized to what they mean.

If your coach uses the following phrases without explaining what's behind them, or offering various ways to communicate a problem or solution, then you're not getting the best lesson you can. Popular go-to coaching phrases include:

- "Stay down with the shot."
- "Carve around the ball" (for a slice serve).
- "Turn the doorknob" (to generate topspin on the forehand).
- "Hit over the top of the ball."
- "Hit below the equator."
- "Brush up."
- "Snap your wrist."
- "Step across on your volley."
- "Step into the ball."

- "Finish high."
- "Bend your knees."
- "Keep your eye on the ball."
- "Follow through."
- "Punch the volley."
- "Watch the ball hit the racket."
- "Knife the ball" (on a backhand slice; like other phrases on this list, it doesn't tell you what to do).

By the way—don't make the mistake of thinking that a coach is only good if he or she played on the pro tour. I currently compete at a 4.5 level. Often, there's even a negative correlation between being an extremely accomplished player and being able to teach the game well, particularly to a beginner, because of what's known as the Curse of Knowledge: The higher a person's ability to execute a task, the lower his ability to explain what he's doing, because it comes automatically to him. A former-pro-player-turned-amateur-coach's ability to play may be so ingrained, and his habits so deeply wired into his subconscious, that he can't help but assume that his students understand what he says instinctively.

How a coach communicates information matters more than the degree to which he can execute a particular movement or stroke. Good coaches know how to prioritize your goals, are willing to see beyond immediate results (or ignore them completely), and have a vision for your overall progress. Think back to the best teachers you ever had, from any subject in school or any sport. What made them so great? What did they say to you, or not say, that allowed you to reach your full potential? These are the same qualities to look for in a coach.

To be clear: I don't blame cookie-cutter teaching pros for coaching the way they do. For the most part, they're responding to what most players want—to get some exercise, have fun, and pick up a few neat tips along the way. Most coaches aren't used to working with students who are serious about improvement and want to leave their comfort zone in favor of new and improved techniques, even if it means spending sixty minutes working on one stroke.

But believe me, nothing makes a coach happier than working with a student who's motivated, engaged, and has a passion for getting better. It makes teaching more fun for them and reminds them why they became a coach. So if you like your current coach but feel the lessons aren't helping you the way they should, speak up and tell your coach what you have in mind. Most likely, he or she will be glad to hear it.

REFLECT

Have an honest conversation with your tennis-playing self. What are your big-picture goals as a player, for real? Are you willing to take several steps back in order to take a giant leap forward? Would you be satisfied with a tennis lesson in which half the time (or more) is spent without even hitting a ball? What type of lesson do you want and need, based on your goals for the future?

32

Doubles Therapy I:
Come Together

If there's one song lyric that explains why a doubles team might not be playing to its full potential, it's Led Zeppelin's "Communication breakdown/Drive me insane."

And if there's a lyric that describes how to make a doubles team stronger, it's the Beatles' "Come together/Right now."

Here's what I mean:

As a doubles player, the relationship you have with your playing partner is like any other relationship in your life. Whether it's a spouse, employee, coworker, or teacher at your child's school, the foundation of that relationship is *communication*. If you've ever been in couples therapy, as I have, you know that a lot of that time is spent learning how to communicate. The partners need to learn, and practice, how to talk and listen, so that both feel acknowledged and heard from their own, unique perspective.

When doubles teams struggle, it's for the same reason. I've observed thousands of amateur doubles teams in my career, and my finding is that most of them don't communicate at all; and if they do, "Which side do you want?" and "Be sure to cover your alley!" are pretty much the extent of it.

The good news is, if you and your doubles partner want to improve your on-court relationship, you don't need hours on the couch with an expensive therapist. All you have to do is come together, like the Beatles say. And I don't mean only a metaphorical "come together and be unified" thing. I'm also talking about a *literal* coming together after every point, in which you and your partner meet at the service line, make eye contact and exchange a fist bump, and unpack the previous point and talk strategy for the next.

Your mid-court conversation can be brief. Something like the following is fine:

Jill: Hey, good thought on that overhead.

Joan: I should've hit it higher.

Jill: No biggie, we'll get 'em next time. What're you thinking now?

Joan: I'll serve wide, then come right up to the net, since they definitely don't like it when we're both up there.

Jill: Great.

When I teach doubles teams how to communicate like this at my clinics, the results are instantaneous and phenomenal.

To start, I have two doubles teams play against each other in a ten-point tiebreak; then, right afterward, I'll speak with one of the teams and ask the players about what happened.

"What do you mean?" they typically reply.

"You guys won 10–7. How?"

They have no idea what I'm talking about. So I walk them through it: Did you hit a lot of winners? Did they make a lot of errors? Did you figure out which player on the other team is weaker and hit mostly at him or her? What causes you to win?

They usually have no clue; all they know is they reached ten points before the other team did, so they won. It's the same with the other team—they don't know why they lost, only that they did.

At this point, I ask them to play another tiebreak. But this time, I tell each team that after every point, they need to come together in the middle of the court, exchange high fives, talk about why they won or lost the last point, and come up with a basic plan for the next one.

Once they start doing this, three things happen. First, both teams *play better,* because they suddenly have a plan and aren't just hitting the ball back in a vacuum, and are noticing which patterns and choices work and which don't. Second, when I debrief them afterward, they can tell me why they won or lost—they're aware of what transpired on the court.

Finally, and best of all, they feel like a team. Before, it was almost like there were two singles matches being played on the same court, but now the partners feel connected, supported, and confident that their partner has their back.

When you pair up to play doubles, you'll face a lot of variables, all of them beyond your control. One partner will have a better serve, one will be more comfortable playing net, one will be more prone to making errors. And let's not forget the biggest variable of all—your opponents, and what they throw at you.

The one thing you and your partner *can* control is how well you operate as a team. Communicating by "coming together" is part of it. Below are some other ingredients you and your teammate should add to your doubles partnership, actions and ideas you can implement to make your double partnership as strong as possible. They apply whether you're in a long-term doubles "marriage," like the Bryan Brothers, or playing with someone new:

Encourage Mutual Action

The biggest deficiency I see in doubles teams is what I call "mutual passivity"—the partners don't strategize, discuss patterns of play, or encourage each other. They're so caught up in the fog of war that they're oblivious to what's happening on court, or that there's someone else on court with them.

Good partners, meanwhile, continually facilitate a sense of "us-ness" through *mutual action*. They support each other, deconstruct previous points, and discuss tactics for the next one. You don't need to be a master of tennis strategy to do this. A single, simple idea about how you might play the upcoming point is enough.

Step Up

Some people like to take the lead; others prefer to hear suggestions and carry them out. Still others would like to take charge but are afraid of sounding bossy. My feeling is, if you're clearly the stronger player—by which I mean, you understand tactics and how to adjust, not necessarily that you have better strokes—you have a responsibility to step up and take the leadership role. Your partner will likely appreciate it.

Give Suggestions, Not Orders

At some point in your doubles career, you've probably been stuck with partners who try to fix your game. They mean well, but their instructions—"Cover your alley!" or "Don't stand there when I poach!" or "Stop hitting it to their net guy!" are common ones—only make you play worse. Plus, you feel humiliated.

I'm not saying you should never give your partner advice. But when you do, make sure you do it in a way that doesn't make her feel untalented, unwanted, or inferior. It comes down to how you communicate the message: Instead of "Don't stand so close to the net!" try "Wow, Sally's hitting some great lobs today. Maybe I'll stand a bit farther back at the net when she's behind the baseline so I can take them out of the air. What do you think?"

By making it clear that you, too, are vulnerable and plan to adjust, you get the result you want from partners without damaging their egos. You also make it seem like you decided on a new tactic together.

Don't Go Negative—Ever!

If you follow only one rule, this is it. Nothing dissolves a doubles partnership faster than negativity. This includes direct criticism—"What's wrong with you?" and "Come on, we needed that point!"—but also indirect criticism, like shaking your head in disbelief, throwing up your hands in disgust, and then walking right past your partner for the next point without acknowledging or supporting him. This passive-aggressive criticism can be the most damaging of all, because it's subtle and secretive, and forces your partner to try to figure out why you're angry.

What if your partner is truly stinking it up? Tearing him to pieces won't make him play better—I guarantee it. If your partner is playing poorly, there are only three possibilities for why: She's trying her best but isn't very good; she's having an off day; or, for whatever reason, she's thrown in the towel and is emotionally disconnected from the match. Criticizing her won't change any of that; if anything, it will make her play worse.

TAKE ACTION

Next time you play doubles, make a conscious effort to connect with your partner after every point. At minimum, make eye contact. Even better, exchange a high five or fist bump and talk strategy for the next point. It might feel strange, but consistent communication is the essential ingredient in every successful doubles team.

Eventually, communicating with your partner like this will become a habit. When it does, it won't be long before you and your partner are singing another song lyric, together. It's the one by Queen. I'm pretty sure you know which one I'm talking about, my friend . . .

33

Doubles Therapy II: Meet My Lesser Half

In a perfect doubles team, each player's strengths make up for the other's weaknesses. Between the two of them, they've got the whole court, and game, covered.

Rarely does it work out that nicely. One player is typically a tiny bit better than the other, which means that your team now has a hole that your opponent can exploit. Still, it may be a very small hole, and one you can cover with intelligent play.

Once in a while, however, you will find yourself paired with a partner who's *significantly* weaker than you—so much weaker that everyone, including your opponent, knows without a doubt that *you* are far and away the better player of the two. The hole in your doubles team is large and glaring. It's a debilitating scenario, because your opponent now has a simple strategy that's both easy to implement and highly effective: "Hit to the weak guy." It works in every situation—if your opponents are on the defensive, they can hit to your partner and reset the point; if they're on offense, they attack your weak partner and put the point away. It doesn't matter how good *you* are; your opponents will avoid you like the plague and pummel your partner, shot after shot, until it's game, set, match.

The weak-doubles-partner scenario might sound hopeless, but it turns out there are a few solutions. Which one you choose depends on two things: how good your opponents are, and their style of doubles play.

Scenario One: Neutral or Weak Opponent

If your opponents are at about the same level as you, weaker, or a tiny bit better, stay the course—you and your partner should play standard doubles. This means each of you covers your assigned sections of the court and pretty much stick to it. When you're up at the net, poach if you can, but don't overdo it. There's no need to be a hero in this situation, because your mediocre opponents won't overrun you.

Scenario Two: Strong Opponents Who Play 1-Up, 1-Back

If your opponents position one player at the net and the other on the baseline, and then stay like that through the entire point, they're giving you a huge gift: You and your partner can now choose which player to hit to, based one which phase of play you're in.

By "phase of play," I mean whether you're in an offensive, defensive, or neutral position. It's a simple system, and goes like this:

If you're in an offensive position and are in clear control of the point, hit toward their net player's side. You've got a golden opportunity to end the point—right here, right now—and hitting to the opponent farther away dramatically increases the chance of the ball coming back again.

If you're on defense or in a neutral position, hit to the player on the baseline. This allows you to extend the point without putting your opponents in an offensive position.

In addition to all this, you, as the stronger player on your team, have another job—to be a boss at the net. This means poaching or fake-poaching on almost every ball that goes to the opposing baseline player. When you do this, you allow yourself to take more balls at the net and potentially end points sooner. You also send a clear message to your opponents that you're a force to be reckoned with and they can't ignore you. This alone can cause them to make mistakes.

Poaching and fake-poaching require quick feet. You need to constantly adjust and readjust your position so you can be in the right place at the right time to receive what you think will be the next incoming shot. Good doubles players make lots of educated guesses about what type of ball they think they'll receive next. Depending on what you foresee, you might leave your section of the court so you can be ready for the upcoming shot.

You might be concerned that leaving your part of the court will lead you to giving up points down the alley. It sometimes will! But it's still the right move. Here's why: If you're aggressive and poach, you might lose, but at least you've given yourselves a fighting chance. If you do nothing, however, your opponents will likely have the upper hand in the match.

In any case, all that matters is that you win more points from poaching and fake-poaching than you lose. My friend and fellow coach Craig O'Shannessy (we met him in chapter 1) came up with a handy way to keep track of the poach vs. points-down-the-alley-lost differential, as follows:

If you poach or fake-poach and the other team hits the ball out or in the net while trying to avoid you, or you hit the ball for a winner, count it as "+1." If they burn you down the alley, that's "−1." Anything else is "0." My philosophy is that you should keep going until you reach −3 or −4, because until then it could be a fluke, and given the matchup and the psychological pressure it puts on your opponent, it's still the smartest play.

Scenario Three: Strong Opponents Who Play 2-Up

I'll cut to the chase: Strong opponents who put both players at the net as soon as they can present your worst-case scenario. Why? Because their 2-up style is structured to attack, and attack they will, the moment they realize your partner is the weak one. In fact, the only time they'll hit to you is when they've got a clear shot for an easy put-away winner; and at that point, you'll feel like a target in a shooting gallery.

In this case, you've got two options. Your best choice, if you can pull it off, is to put yourself in an offensive position before your opponents can, and disrupt their ability to take over the match. Doing this requires that you, as the stronger player, be a monster at the net. No more waiting for weak floaters, no hoping to be involved in the point—it's time to poach, fake-poach, and close in tight on every possible shot. When it's your turn to serve, it's serve-and-volley; when you receive, hit a clean return to their server and then close in on the net.

Consider yourself warned: You will lose more points down the alley when you're this aggressive at the net. But if you lose, at least you'll go down fighting. And you never know—it might work.

Option two is to simply commit to defense and play 2-back—you and your partner position yourselves on the baseline and stay there the entire match. I'm not a big fan of this, because you're essentially handing complete control of the match to your opponents; the only way you'll win is if they self-implode (which is a possibility). So start with the first option, and if you get beaten bad, switch to 2-back and play defense—at that point, it's your only hope.

I want to mention that the hardest part about playing 2-back is the psychological hurdle associated with doing so. Doubles players tend to regard 2-back as a lesser and less evolved form of tennis, right up there with serving underhand.

It's not. Pro teams play 2-back all the time when they find themselves getting beat up at the net. (I've included video of this in the online content for this chapter.) There's no shame in playing 2-back, particularly when the only other option is to stand like a human target in the service box while your opponents hammer away.

TAKE ACTION

Progression 1

Go online and watch professional and high-level amateur doubles matches (5.0 and up), and then watch a few low-level matches (2.5 and 3.0). Compare the targets they hit to, what portions of the court they cover and choose to leave open, and how often they do or don't move.

Also note how low-level players don't differentiate between being in offensive vs. defensive phases of play, and thus waste opportunities to attack. High-level teams, meanwhile, are always on the move—both players cover multiple sections of the court, intercept shots ahead of time, and move early as a way to fake out opponents and draw shots to their side of the court.

Progression 2

Use Craig's +1/–1 tally when you poach/fake-poach. Keep track of whether or not poaching/faking pays off.

You can, and should, use +1/–1 in singles matches, too—not only for net play, but with any aggressive, out-of-the-box choice you might make, like hitting an aggressive second serve or utilizing a serve-and-volley. So long as you're winning as many points as you lose, it makes sense to keep doing it. Even if you're not gaining lots of points, it plants a seed of doubt in your opponents' minds and gives them one more thing to worry about.

THE
MENTAL
GAME

34

Mental Tennis Lies: Cry, Baby, Cry

*"I was really nervous like never before . . .
Five minutes before the match, I started to cry."*

The above quote is from a tennis player, describing how he felt before an important match against a tough opponent.

You might assume the player in question was an elementary school kid, or maybe a high schooler before the state finals. In fact, it was Stan Wawrinka—at the time, the No. 5 player in the world and a two-time Grand Slam champion, recounting how he felt before the 2016 US Open final against Novak Djokovic.

It's worth noting that at this point in his career, Wawrinka was thirty-one years old, had been playing tennis for twenty-three years, and had already won the French and

Australian Opens and an Olympic gold medal. He'd seen his fair share of big matches and won. He had no reason in the world to cry. Yet cry he did. He was also "completely shaking" in the locker room as he sat there with his coach, Magnus Norman. That's how nervous he was before the match.

Moral of the story: Even the most accomplished players in the world get nervous. So, if you find yourself crying and shaking and your heart is racing before a match, don't fret: You're not alone.

That said, there is one very big difference between Stan Wawrinka's anxiety and yours. I want to debunk four very big lies about mental toughness and the psychological aspect of the game.

1. **Lie 1: Good players don't get nervous.** Our man Wawrinka proved that they do. And he is not an outlier. Federer, Serena, Djokovic, and Nadal all readily admit to feeling nervous before and during their play. So do Hall of Fame athletes in other sports, including NBA great Bill Russell and NFL quarterback Jim Kelly, both of whom would get sick to their stomachs before games.

2. **Lie 2: If you're nervous, that means you're not mentally tough.** The players I mentioned, particularly Nadal, are some of the most mentally tough in the game. As you'll soon see, it's not the absence of anxiety, fear, and doubt that makes you mentally

tough, but how you react to anxiety when it presents itself.

3. **Lie 3: You're either mentally tough or you're not.** Mental toughness isn't something you're born with. It can be learned, developed, and practiced, like your ground stroke. (In the next chapter, we'll talk about how.)

4. **Lie 4: If you're nervous, that means there's something wrong with you.** This might be the most dangerous lie of all, and why the mental side of tennis is such a train wreck for so many. It's a self-defeating cycle: Players assume they shouldn't be nervous; when they inevitably are, they interpret their nervousness as evidence that there's something wrong with them—they're unprepared, they're psychologically weak, they lack confidence. They also assume their anxiety will cause them to play worse. So they try to fix the situation by getting rid of the anxiety, typically by telling themselves lies they don't believe ("There's nothing to be nervous about; it's just a stupid tennis match") or by focusing on calming but ridiculous imagery (sunsets, puppy dogs, hot-air balloons) that has nothing to do with the match they're about to play, in the hopes that the nervousness will go away . . . which of course it doesn't . . . and this makes them even more nervous . . .

What I want you to realize is that *it's okay to feel*

nervous! I think it's good when a player feels nervous before a match—it means he or she cares. Here's how Federer describes it:

> "I do get nervous—and I'm happy that I do for the big occasions . . . because it means I care. It's not like going through the motions, like being careless—that would be a horrible feeling."

So, let's say you're about to play a match and you feel nervous. You know the signs—heart is thumping, throat is tight, muscles are tense. Totally normal, but not the ideal way to play a tennis match. So what do you do?

When you feel anxious, you have two choices for how to respond:

Response 1: "I'm nervous. Oh, no!"

This is how most amateur athletes respond, and even many pros. They feel anxious, assume that anxiety is bad, and immediately start thinking about either the past or the future. Future thoughts include things like, "If I lose, I'll feel humiliated" or "I want to beat him so badly. What if I don't?" Past-oriented thoughts center on things that have already happened, including past failures ("I lost last time; I hope I don't lose again!") and, believe it or not, past successes ("I crushed her last week; if she wins, that means my victory was a fluke!").

What all of these thoughts have in common is that they're about a period of time other than the only time that truly matters—*now*. Your game plan for the match, your intentions, your targets, your strategies, your opponent's weaknesses, and ways to capitalize on them—these are the things you should think about as you get ready to play. Anything else is a distraction.

Response 2: "I'm nervous. Oh, yeah!"

Believe it or not, elite athletes relish feeling nervous. Why? Because anxiety means one thing: *This is what it's all about!* All the training, the physical and mental exertion, the exhaustion after hours on the court and in the gym—this moment, right now, is what it's all for. Here's the second part of Wawrinka's quote, about how he reacted to his US Open pre-match anxiety:

> "The only thing I was convinced with myself was that my game was there. Physically, I was there. My game was there. Just put the fight on the court, and [I] will have a chance to win."

And he did: Wawrinka defeated then–World No. 1 Djokovic in four sets to capture the 2016 US Open title.

TAKE ACTION

To become mentally tough, you need to change how you think about anxiety. From now on, try to see nervousness as something good. This means flipping the switch from "Oh, no, I'm nervous!" to "Oh, yeah, it's go time!"

This is a drastic attitude change and won't happen by

accident. You need to practice this response like you'd practice hitting backhands at half-speed.

Progression 1

Place yourself in a situation where something's on the line—
your reputation, money, victory in a competition—and your
performance at least partially determines the outcome. This
can be on the tennis court or off.

For example: if, like most people, you don't enjoy public
speaking, offer to give a short presentation to your colleagues
at work. Chances are that before your talk, you'll feel quite
nervous; when you do, remind yourself that it's because you
care—and that this is a fantastic opportunity to test yourself
and improve your skills.

Progression 2

Look back on the last six to twelve months of your life and try
to recall those scenarios that brought you the most mental an-
guish, either on the court or off. Is there a pattern? Do certain
situations continually make you feel nervous? How did you
react to the anxiety in each situation? If these scenarios were to
occur now, would you react the same way? Differently?

Progression 3

Call up the tennis player you least enjoy playing against because the thought of losing to this person is simply
unbearable—and schedule a match. When you feel nervous
before the match (as you certainly will), greet your anxiety

with a big "Oh, yes! This is what it's all about, baby!" Then play the best tennis that you possibly can.

If you win, congratulations! Relish the feeling of success.

If you lose, congratulations! You did something 99 percent of your peers aren't willing to do—you sought out discomfort, did your best in a challenging environment, and came away a stronger, more experienced competitor. I'm proud of you for taking that powerful step toward better tennis.

35

Mental Tennis Truths: Emotional Shadow Swings

In the previous chapter, I exposed four very big mental tennis lies.

But what about mental tennis truths? All tennis players want to be mentally tough, but what does "mental toughness" look like?

Most players have no idea. And to be completely honest with you, for pretty much all of my playing career, I didn't either. "It's key to keep your cool" is what I probably would have said in high school and college. "You don't throw your racket or scream at the umpire. And you don't get nervous before a match." (We already saw that this last one's not true.)

Once I started Essential Tennis, however, I saw firsthand how many students wanted, needed, *craved* advice on the mental side of the game. So I stepped away from the court and consulted with sports psychologists and mental toughness gurus, foremost among them Ed Tseng.

Ed is an expert on peak performance and author of the book *Game. Set. Life.* He's dedicated his career to helping people achieve their fullest potential in a way that leads them to feel both happy and fulfilled. I credit him with teaching me an important idea about the mental side of the game: that mental toughness can be taught, learned, and practiced like any other skill. It's not a case of "You either got it or you don't."

So how do you go about getting mentally stronger?

As it turns out, you develop mental toughness the same way you'd develop a high-level forehand or any other stroke. You start by identifying what the ideal version of the skill or stroke looks like. You practice it in step-by-step progressions, in a controlled environment, and then slowly add in more variables until the skill becomes hardwired into a habit. Finally, you incorporate the new skill into competitive play.

This completely changed my concept of being "mentally tough." I realized that most tennis players, including myself, never bother doing the first step—we'll watch slow-motion video of Federer's forehand for hours, but we don't spend any time thinking about what good mental toughness looks or feels like. Nor do we set aside time to train it. Instead, we think of mental toughness as something you develop on the court, in the heat of the moment (if it can be developed at all).

Here's the problem: If you wait until you're playing a match to try to be mentally tough, it's too late. Once the match is under way, you'll be caught up in the emotions swirling inside you. You won't be able to react, think, and behave in the way you ideally want.

Based on my work with Ed and conversations with other tennis and mental health professionals, I've distilled the essential principles of mental toughness into a simple, actionable three-step process:

Step 1: Reflection. In a quiet place, away from the court, meditate on the idea of mental toughness. "See" mental toughness in your head. What does it look like?

To stimulate your imagination, I've listed some situations below that tend to cause players to get emotional, along with possible reactions for the first few. Picture yourself in each scenario. Then see yourself reacting the way you truly want to. What's your ideal response to each?

There are, of course, no right or wrong answers. This exercise is purely subjective—the point is to put you in touch with your best version of your mentally tough self.

- You lose an important point.

  Do you laugh and shake it off? Shout or curse, then immediately drop it and get back to business? Stare at the strings of your racket for three seconds, then move on?

- You win an important point.

  Do you celebrate with a loud "Come on!" Pump your fist? Utter a quiet "Nice!" to yourself? Or perhaps experience no reaction at all and just proceed to the next point?

- Your opponent hits a beautiful winner and celebrates with an unsportsmanlike outburst—he looks right at you, pumps his fist, and shouts, "That's what I'm talking about!"

  Do you stare him down? Chuckle? Whisper, "What a weirdo," and turn your back? Applaud his great shot with a thumbs-up or racket-clap? Ignore him completely?

- You blow an easy shot.
- You double-fault.
- Your opponent jumps to a 4-games-to-0 lead.
- You jump out to a big lead.
- It's a third-set tiebreak and you're serving for match point.
- Same as above . . . but you're receiving.
- Like the previous two . . . but now your opponent has match point.

As you ponder these possible situations, think about your inner dialogue as well.

What's your ideal version of self-talk? Do you criticize yourself, or speak only positively? Is the purpose of your self-talk mostly to pump yourself up, or is it to correct tactical and technical errors? Or perhaps, when you're in your ideal mental state, you don't talk to yourself at all?

Finally, think about how you want yourself to play the most important points of a match—game and break points, set points, and match point.

Do you play all out?

Hold back and play it safe?

Hit with the same swing speed or a bit slower or faster?

Play to win, or to not lose?

Step 2: Emotional Shadow Swings. Now that you're in touch with how you *want* to react and behave, you need to practice these responses with what I call "emotional shadow swings."

Emotional shadow swings are like the shadow swings you do to improve a forehand: slow and steady repetitions, with all outside variables removed. There's no outcome you're trying to attain or avoid, no pressure to get it "right." It's simply a chance to practice the most basic elements of your new skill.

To do a mental-toughness shadow swing, start by thinking about the three or four on-court situations that bother you most. These will be different for every player. You're looking for the scenarios that, based on experience, you know are most likely to make you lose your cool.

Now picture yourself in each of these stressful situations.

See yourself reacting the way you want to react. Spend a few minutes on each scenario before moving on to the next one. A few days later, pick three or four other bothersome situations and see yourself responding how you want to in each. And so on.

Step 3: Mental Toughness in Competition. Being mentally tough on your sofa is one thing; staying strong in a match is another. To practice mental toughness when it counts, you need to do something you might not want to: intentionally place yourself in stressful situations, both on the court and off, so you can practice responding the way you want to, outside of a controlled environment.

Off-court stressful situations might include waiting your turn at the DMV, heading to the grocery store during peak hours and purposely choosing the longest checkout line, and driving in stop-and-go rush-hour traffic. What these situations all have in common is that there's a desired outcome (get your car registration processed, pay for your groceries, arrive at your destination) and obstacles that stand in the way—obstacles that you cannot control. In each situation, practice responding and behaving the way you visualized ahead of time.

Competing head-to-head against other tennis players on court is a great way to build mental toughness. But fortunately (or not), everyday life provides plenty of other opportunities for you to practice your ideal version of "mentally tough." Embrace these frustrating situations as opportunities to grow.

It's possible your ideal version of mental toughness isn't the one that helps you play your best. You might assume, for example, that remaining stone-faced and calm after blowing an easy shot is the "correct" reaction, but perhaps a quick outburst would allow you to discharge whatever negative energy you've got pent up inside you and allow you to perform better. There's this notion that the more emotion a player exhibits, the less mentally tough he or she is. When a professional player shouts, screams, or smashes his or her racket into the ground, we interpret their outbursts as evidence that they've lost control and aren't mentally tough. But it could be that these players, most of whom have been competing at a high level for a decade or more, have discovered that they play best when they allow themselves to periodically blow off some steam—it's simply their version of what's ideally "mentally tough" for them.

That said, I've met only one player who performed better when he was in an all-out angry state, John McEnroe–style. My college teammate Jason would often walk to a corner between points and curse himself and work himself into an angry fit, then use his anger as fuel for the next point. In his case, it worked—he played his best when he was furious.

If you're one of those rare people for whom anger makes you play better, so be it—you hereby have my permission to stomp, shout, and whine to your heart's content, so long as you don't disrespect your opponent, damage property, or serve as a bad example to kids who happen to be watching.

In general, though, I've found that when players are angry, they perform worse—*much* worse. I therefore don't recommend it.

36

Dealing with McEnroes (and Lawn Mowers, and Babies, and Nadals)

What do John McEnroe, a baby, and a lawn mower have in common?

It sounds like one of those strange mythological riddles. But it's a serious question, especially if you intend to stay focused for the duration of an entire match.

The answer?

Each is a potential distraction. Whether it's an opponent who smashes his racket into the fence, a park employee who decides to trim the grass the moment you step to the line to serve, or a crying baby nearby, these and other outside forces can break your concentration and cause you to shift your focus away from the only thing that matters—the upcoming point.

Players mistakenly believe that the solution to a distraction is to somehow *make the distraction go away,* or to simply *pretend it's not there.* If only that baby would stop crying, if only that guy would turn off his phone, everything would be okay. This mode of thinking is common at every level, from beginning players and up through the WTA and ATP Tours.

As a result, players waste an enormous amount of mental and physical energy trying to change whatever circumstance is bothering them. Either that, or they stew quietly behind the baseline, suddenly obsessed with whatever or whoever is causing the problem.

Here's what I mean:

For any given distraction, you have two choices: *Am I going to allow this to bother me? Or not?*

The answer is clear: You cannot allow the distraction to get to you. If you do, you're done.

Why?

Because mental focus is exactly like visual focus. At any given time, your field of vision encompasses about 170 degrees—but what you see *clearly* is restricted to a 6-degree slice of that entire field. Although you're "seeing" a lot, you can *focus* on only one thing at a time.

It's the same with your brain. Although ideas and thoughts might be stampeding through your mind, you can truly focus on only one of them. That's why "multitasking" is a myth. To paraphrase a popular quote, multitasking is just messing up a bunch of things at once. To perform a task well, you need to focus completely and singularly on that one task.

How does this play out on the tennis court? To put it simply, at any given moment, you're either focused on the point you're about to play or you're not. Period. So once you start brooding about that line call your opponent missed on the previous point, or you catch a glimpse of your opponent setting up his water bottle just so, a la Rafael Nadal, during a changeover and you start wondering who he thinks he is, anyway, and why he doesn't just play tennis . . . you are now, by definition, *not* thinking about tactics, targets, and intentions for the upcoming point. (Online, there's great footage of Nadal's opponents knocking over his water bottles in frustration. Nadal has many quirky routines, all of them potentially distracting to insecure opponents.)

Distractions come in many flavors. Every tennis player has his or her own set of triggers that set him or her off. Most are related to your opponent's behavior, but some are not.

We'll look at a list of common distractions, then discuss how to maintain focus in the face of these disturbances.

I'd love to hear of additional distractions, ones you've faced in your own tennis career. Please share them in the Facebook group linked in the online content for this chapter.

- **Meltdowns.** Your opponent throws a tantrum, McEnroe-style—complete with swearing, racket-smashing, knocking over chairs, or worse.
- **Outbursts.** It's perfectly fine to shout, "Come on!" or

"What was I thinking?" every once in a while. But some opponents go berserk after every point.

- **Scorekeepers.** "Second serve," your opponent calls out after you missed your first. *No kidding!* you think. These same folks call out the score before every point, even when they're not serving.

- **Commentary.** I'm talking about opponents who channel their inner Mary Carillo throughout the entire match. They're super complimentary of your shots, offer advice when you make an error, and provide TV-style commentary after points: "Wow, nice backhand, I didn't think you'd reach it because you seemed off balance . . ."

- **Technically legal but definitely nonstandard behaviors.** Nadal can't serve or receive a ball unless he first touches his forehead, tugs his shorts, wipes behind each ear . . . Other players bounce the ball an inordinate number of times before serving; at the recreational level, players take calls on their cell phones between points or bring their young children to the match and discipline them throughout ("Sit still, Jimmy!").

- **Annoying fans.** Your opponent brings an entourage of cheerleaders. It's bad enough they cheer every time he wins a point; what's worse is that they also applaud your errors and double faults.

- **Noise.** A park employee revs up his 200-horsepower leaf blower to clear the sidewalk next to your court.

The players on the court next to you carry on a running conversation about the upcoming election. A guy strolls around talking into his mobile on speaker-phone while children scurry about screaming at the top of their lungs . . .

- **Blown calls.** If your opponent calls your shot out when you clearly saw it was in, you have every right to question it. But it's ultimately his call. One bad call rarely determines the outcome of a match. Continuing to brood over a bad call will.

- **Foot faults.** If your opponent foot-faults, you can either call it yourself or, if you're playing a tournament, notify a roaming judge. That said, I wouldn't let foot faults bother you, nor do I suggest you call them—they indicate poor balance and faulty mechanics. *Thinking* about your opponent's foot faults, however, is a major distraction that many players get obsessed with. But that's all it is—a distraction.

I realize that ignoring these disturbances is easier said than done. "Don't let it get to you" is pretty cheap advice—when an opponent or circumstance gets under your skin, it's hard to drop it.

But you must. The following three-step process, which I call "The 3 As," will show you how:

1. **Acknowledge** that something is distracting you. Don't lie to yourself—better to acknowledge the

truth—that your attention is being pulled away—so you can handle it properly.

2. **Accept** the undeniable fact that this circumstance is beyond your control. Since you can't do anything about it anyway, you might as well not think about it. After all, if you can't control the distraction, why allow the distraction to control you?

3. **Alter** your focus, consciously redirecting it to what matters: strategy, patterns of play, your opponent's weaknesses, and your intention for the match.

One of the reasons I find tennis so fascinating is that it's not just about skill, but a battle between two distinct personalities. Which personality is best suited to handle the unexpected circumstances that come up? Whose energy level and mental fortitude will persevere?

Sometimes the true winner of a tennis match isn't the player who ends up with the trophy, but the one who persevered despite the obstacles. There is such a thing as a personal win. So, when you score one, don't dismiss it. Sometimes these personal wins matter most.

TAKE ACTION

Progression 1

Part of what makes distractions annoying is that they're unexpected. The solution: Expect distractions to happen.

In your tennis journal, list all the things that tend to distract you during a match. List them in order, most annoying to least. Include circumstances you faced in the past, as well as new ones you can imagine might bug you.

Then consider your ideal response to each. What reactions will allow you to play the best tennis you can and allow you to maintain your concentration?

Progression 2

The next time you play a match and a distraction comes up, practice your premeditated reaction. Did your planned response allow you to play differently than if you'd simply reacted the way you normally do?

Progression 3

Schedule a match when you know there will be distractions around—perhaps during Moms-and-Tots tennis time or pee-wee classes, or against an opponent who's notorious for foot-faulting, missing line calls, throwing tantrums . . . or, if you're lucky, all three.

Practice using the Three As.

37

Managing Tennis Energy: Intensity

When you play tennis, how much time is spent actually *playing tennis*?

I've done the math. Assuming it takes about two hours to play a full three-set match, my best estimate is that the total amount of time playing points is, at most, thirty minutes. And that's a conservative estimate: I assumed long rallies, several multiple-deuce games, and all three sets finishing 6–4. In reality, your true playing time would probably be twenty-five minutes or less. (You can experience this for yourself by recording a close set of match play and editing the footage to remove all the downtime.)

In any case, it's not the actual number that matters, but the idea: Three-quarters of any given tennis match is spent doing things other than playing tennis!

It's absurd when you think about it. What exactly is going on during that 75 percent of the time when you're not playing? It leads to the question: What should you be doing, and what should you be thinking about, during all that time when the ball isn't in play?

It's an important question. Because what you do between points is as important as what you do during the points themselves.

Here's how it breaks down:

During the three to ten seconds it takes to play a typical point, you want to operate at *peak intensity*. You're fully alert. You are completely engaged. You are *locked in*. You expend every ounce of physical and mental energy you have to track the ball, move explosively, hit to your target, and recover in time for the next incoming shot. So long as the ball is in play, *you are 100 percent on*.

Then, when the point ends, you shut it off—completely. If you need to blow off some steam, then shout, yell, stomp your feet—and quickly move on. You relax your mind and body. Whatever emotional drama you experienced during the previous point, you drop it—completely disengage. Your mind is like the surface of a country lake at dawn—tranquil, smooth, quiet.

In the twenty seconds between points, should you think at all? Yes, but gently. Calmly, and without judgment, reflect on how the previous point ended and whether it's part of an overall pattern you can exploit. Consider your intention for the point you're about to play. But otherwise, *you are 100 percent off.*

And then: You step to the baseline and completely reengage for the next point, *100 percent on.*

It goes back and forth like this for the entire match: totally on, totally off. Absolute intensity, zero intensity.

The alternative to this is what most club-level players and even some pros do: They carry their emotions from the previous point into the break and on into the next point. They remain riled up at their peak level of intensity. But nobody can maintain peak emotional and physical intensity for an entire match. Before long, these players get burned out—they have nothing left to give.

An unfortunate example of this is Nick Kyrgios. Many knowledgeable tennis professionals, myself included, believe that Kyrgios has what it takes to reach World No. 1. But over and over, his tools and talent are hijacked by his on-court antics—he's simply too emotionally charged between points. Watch a Kyrgios match online and notice how often he refuses to let go of the point that just happened. While his opponent waits calmly on the other side of the net, Kyrgios curses, gesticulates, and hurls criticism at his opponent, the umpire, and himself. It's impossible to perform one's best and maintain a high level of play for a whole match under these circumstances.

TAKE ACTION

Next time you play a match, or even hit with a friend, practice being fully engaged during points and then disengaging in between. Do you find yourself playing better when you allow yourself the mental and physical space to decompress? What do you notice about the quality and quantity of your energy during and after the match?

38

Second-Set Slump

One of my absolute favorite things to do is wade into the ocean and stand in the exact spot where the waves break. As each swell comes surging toward me, I know I have a choice: dive down and let the wave crash over me, or stand still and get knocked over.

Similarly, the momentum of a tennis match shifts back and forth between players or teams over the course of the match. Unfortunately, it's hard to know exactly when momentum shifts are about to happen—except for one. I'm talking about the one momentum swing that's pretty much guaranteed to happen every single match, and always at the exact same time—right after the conclusion of the first set. I'm referring to how, very often, a player will win the first set of a match, only to lose the second. It's such a common phenomenon that I've given it a name: the Second-Set Slump. It happens for the same reason people might get knocked off their feet in the ocean—they fail to see that there's a tidal wave on the horizon, about to alter the landscape.

Why is there almost always a momentum shift after the first set? Quite simply, because your opponent knuckles down and commits to doing whatever it takes to win the next set—especially because she now has nothing to lose. She's mulling over your weaknesses and putting together a game plan. And as the victor of the first set, you need to do the exact same thing.

Instead, after most players win the first set, they do the following:

1. **Celebrate.** *This one's in the bag,* you say to yourself. Who cares that you still need to win another set—you've already popped open the champagne. Your mind wanders. You think about how great it's going to feel to shake hands with your opponent at the net, the way he's going to congratulate you. You feel glad you invested in that ball machine . . .

    When the second set begins, your lack of focus combined with your opponent's heightened concentration allow your opponent to jump out to an early lead. By the time you realize what's happening, it's too late: one set apiece.

2. **Panic.** Sometimes winning the first set fills you with dread. *Last time we played, I won the opening set and then blew it,* you recall. *What if that happens again?*

   And it does, because instead of playing to win, you play to avoid losing. You shorten your stroke and decelerate on your swings in an effort to control your shots. You feel anxious and tight. The tension restricts your ability to move, swing freely, and hit with power.

   Your opponent, meanwhile, is honed. He notices your tentative game plan and easily attacks your shots. He takes the set before you realize what hit you.

3. **Fail to adjust.** If your opponent is any good at all, he won't simply go down with the ship. He'll redouble his efforts and put together a plan to cut down on his errors and capitalize on your weaknesses. He might even decide to try something wildly different—serve-and-volley instead of grinding it out from the baseline, for example, or hit exclusively to your backhand.

   You should do the same. Just because your tactics worked in the first set doesn't automatically mean they'll work in the second. Reflect on what patterns of play were and were not successful. Assume that your opponent is going to play this next set differently. What might he do, and when he does, how will you react?

As you may have noticed, the Second-Set Slump happens for the same reason all mental breakdowns do—the player thinks about the past or future, instead of staying focused on *now*. It calls to mind one of my pastor's favorite expressions: "There are two days you should never obsess about—yesterday and tomorrow."

Or, in tennis terms, the point you just played and the one after the one you're playing now.

TAKE ACTION

Play a match. Regardless of who won the first set, use the pause between sets to reevaluate your tactics and consider how your opponent might surprise you in the upcoming set. As you do this, make a conscious effort to stay grounded in the moment and think about the only thing that matters: the upcoming set.

Conclusion

"Finding Fulfillment: Love for the Tennis Journey"

I recently ran into one of my former students. We caught up for a few minutes. Then I asked how his tennis was coming along, and he smiled. "I don't play," he said. He explained that at some point, the game had stopped being fun. He'd gotten sick of it—sick of making the same mistakes and losing to the same people. Sick of practicing and trying so hard to improve, only to play a match and have it all fall apart. Even when he won, it felt like a struggle. As he said all of this, he looked genuinely happy—and relieved—that tennis was no longer part of his life.

I asked if he'd taken up another sport. "I run," he said. "And I love it. Because unless it starts raining or I step in dog crap, I know I'm going to enjoy it. It was never like that with tennis."

I can't say I was shocked to hear he'd quit. Surprised, maybe. But not shocked. A lot of serious players I know have at some point thought about quitting. The feeling typically doesn't last—maybe as long as the car ride home after a bad loss. But I do know players who quit for a few months or even years. Once in a while, a player quits for good.

Believe me, I get it. Tennis can be excruciating. The game is designed to accentuate your flaws. And the failure rate is incredibly high: Even when playing your best, you're going to lose almost half the points. And since 70 percent of all points end with an error, you're pretty much guaranteed to make a mistake on one out of every three points. Only a masochist would attempt to enjoy an activity in which he screws up a third of time.

Among the many things I hope you got out of this book is an appreciation of just how often you succeed in the face of so many obstacles. Just hitting a ground stroke or volley in the court is an impressive feat. Don't take it for granted.

I also want you to appreciate just how little you can actually control once you're out on the court. One of the biggest myths in tennis is that a player can control how well he or she plays. In fact, you can only control three things: your attitude; your effort level, or intensity; and what you choose to focus on versus ignore. Everything else—sun, wind, noise, the speed and spin of your opponent's ground strokes, the fairness (or lack thereof) of your opponent's line calls, how well your opponent plays, and everything else—is 100 percent beyond your control.

"What about technique?" you might ask. "I might not be able to control the weather, but surely I can control my footwork, whether I keep my head still at contact, and where I toss the ball on my serve—right?"

Believe it or not, these things are also beyond your complete control. You can practice them—and you should. But on any given day, your ability fluctuates. Some days, your timing will be spectacular; others, it'll be off. We've all had days when, for no apparent reason, the racket feels foreign in our hands and we can't hit a ball in to save our life.

Nor can you fully control the inordinate number of tiny elements that make up a particular stroke or movement— the racket takeback and drop, the contact point, the position of your torso and head, and so on—especially under pressure. How well you execute your swing and your strategy changes from match to match, from set to set, and even from one point to the next. There are simply too many variables in play.

Does it ever happen that all the various aspects of your game come together and you play your absolute best? Sure. About three or four times a year. Any other time, you step out there with less than a full box of tools.

The only reason I know any of this is because I experienced it myself. Senior year of college, I quit the team and walked away from playing the game competitively. For ten years, tennis had been the thing that brought me the most happiness in life, but suddenly, I was miserable—the result of a gap between my expectation that I should play at a certain level and the reality of how little I could actually control. I found myself trudging off to practice reluctantly, wondering why I was even doing it. One day, I decided that if it didn't make me happy, I shouldn't.

All told, I was away from the competitive side of tennis for four years. It was during this time that I began my full-time coaching career. The combination of the two—not competing and helping others—allowed me to heal my relationship with the game, and with myself. For the first time in my life, I was able to define myself beyond how well I performed on court. Ironically, it was only by walking away from the game competitively that I found out what tennis meant to me and whether the game belonged in my life.

The moral of the story is not that you should quit playing tennis! It's that if you do find yourself at a crossroads, allow yourself some space. Unplug for a few weeks. Decompress. Let your body and mind reset, *then* see how you feel. Figure out what tennis means to you, like I did, and how your relationship with the game can be healthy. And never forget the one and only reason any of us play: because it makes us happy.

That's not to say that every moment on the court is going

to be bliss. To truly enjoy the game, you need to enjoy the full spectrum of what tennis has to offer. This means embracing the highs *and* the lows, as well as all the wonderful benefits our sport has to offer—like discipline, perseverance, mental focus, self-exploration, physical health, and social interaction. These are some of the reasons we pursue hobbies of any kind. That tennis gives us all of them is a testament to how personally enriching the game is. If you do take a break, I hope you return.

One of the best ways to understand the full experience of tennis is to watch the trophy ceremony at the end of a Grand Slam. You'll most likely see two people crying. For the player who lost, it's because she came incredibly close to achieving a lifelong dream but fell short. For the winner, it's because she's realizing the fulfillment of that same lifelong dream, and the culmination of countless hours of pain, sacrifice, and failure that were required to get there. Even if you could avoid the pain, would you really want to? You'd leave so much on the table—the growth, the sense of personal development, and the pride of achievement that comes with overcoming obstacles. Genuine fulfillment is what makes the journey worthwhile.

My wish for you is that you experience the full range of this incredible game. When you embrace the struggle of tennis with the right perspective, every little positive step signifies personal growth. In my opinion, tennis is the most wonderful way to engage your mind, body, and spirit for a happy and fulfilling life.

Transformation Stories

Case Study 1: Feel Versus Real

When it comes to amateur tennis players, there are those who enjoy the game and those who are obsessed. My student Rob is one of the obsessed ones. Born, raised, and currently living in Detroit, he belongs to two (yes, two) tennis clubs, just so he can be sure to get a court during vicious Michigan winters.

Rob is a 4.0 player in his forties. He came to me because he wanted to develop an offensive weapon—a shot or shots that would help him put opponents away and end points on his terms.

After a couple minutes of light sparring, I recognized exactly what was holding Rob back: He hit with tons of topspin, but had no ability to drive *through* the ball with power. Topspin is what keeps the ball in the court, and it causes the ball to kick up after it lands, but too much topspin leads to short ground strokes that bounce around the service line. So it was with Rob. His ground strokes were high and spinny. When he won points, it was because his opponents screwed up, not because Rob hit a winner.

Using video, Rob and I discovered that his normal swing path was *so* vertical (low-to-high) that it had virtually no horizontal component. Even when he attempted to swing flat, he still swung up at about a 40-degree angle.

To get him to swing flat, I used one of my favorite techniques: tricking students into using correct technique. Instead of asking Rob to swing flat, I instructed him to swing high-to-low. It was only after being asked for an extreme downward swing that he finally leveled things out and succeeded in hitting a solid drive. And in hitting winners that put opponents away.

Case Study 2: Effortless Power

Meet Jina—a 3.0 player in her forties from California. An Essential Tennis fan for many years, Jina flew out to Wisconsin to work with me personally because, in her words, "I'm ready to take my game to the next level." I thought, *Good for her!*

When a player plays 3.0, there are obviously many things she might do to improve her game. But I always try to look for what I call the One Big Thing that will make the biggest impact in the least amount of time. In this case, Jina's One Big Thing was learning how to use her body correctly to create power. In our opening hit-around, Jina hit forehands with a tight, jerky swing that had barely any force behind it. She'd attempted to fix this herself by swinging harder, but the more effort she exerted, the more mistakes she made, and her forehand fell apart.

In order to improve, Jina had to learn how to reverse the way she used her body throughout the stroke. Instead of her arm working hard and her body being passive, I taught her how to let the big muscles of her body do the work and allow her arm to "come along for the ride."

The end result, for Jina and others who have learned how to let their legs and trunk do the work, was smooth, calm, effortless power.

Watch my lesson with Jina here:

Case Study 3: There Is No Ball

Sometimes a student has good technical fundamentals but, for whatever reason, just can't hit the ball with power. Such was the case with Justin—a 3.5 player in his forties from Utah. Justin came to me with a very specific goal: He wanted to beat his longtime nemesis, who had a worse-looking game but never lost.

Unlike many students, Justin actually used his body well, had a good contact position, and prepared early. So what was holding him back?

Neither he nor I could tell during our warm-up. But after watching slow-motion video of his forehand, we discovered that at the very last moment before contact, Justin tightened his entire arm—biceps, forearm, wrist, and fingers—in an effort to exert a last-second dose of power on the ball and steer it to his intended target. Unfortunately, the result of this tension is less control and less power, not more—because flexing your muscles actually slows down the racket!

My goal for Justin was simple: to get him to relax! I worked him through a series of drills that helped him release tension until, finally, he was playing loose—for the first time in his tennis-playing life.

The happy result was more accuracy and power on his stroke with far less effort.

And yes—within a month, Justin started beating his long-time rival.

Check out our session here:

Case Study 4: Tennis IQ

Club-level players put a lot of emphasis on technique. But I've always believed that just as important is what we coaches call Tennis IQ—the degree to which a player understands patterns of play and which types of shots to hit in a given situation.

Phil, a thirty-five-year-old 4.0 player from California, had a high Tennis IQ, but come match time, "chose" to hit shots that made no sense. I put the word "chose" in quotes because in reality he wasn't choosing to hit any particular shot at all; he just hit the ball back to his opponent without thinking. Instead of playing high-percentage tennis, he tried to hit winners from defensive positions and aimed for small, risky targets that inevitably led to unforced errors. Not surprisingly, Phil often lost to opponents with less technical skill and fewer tools than he had.

When putting together my lesson plan for Phil, I decided that in order to take him forward, I would first need to take him several steps back. This meant implementing a rigid structure around shot selection that he was required to follow until, with enough practice, he'd be able to pick smart, appropriate targets automatically.

See my lesson with Phil here:

Case Study 5: First and Second Serve

Audrey is a 3.0 player from Colorado. She came to me with the hope that we'd take her entire game to the next level. I chose to start with her serve—the one shot over which she (and every other player) has complete control.

Audrey had a good first serve. Her second, however, was nothing but a dramatically slower version of her first. Or, to phrase it less politely, she barely had any second serve at all.

Audrey's problem is a common one at the 3.0 and 3.5 levels: Players choose to "play it safe" by tapping a soft, gentle serve to start the point and avoid double-faulting. To do this, they slow down their racket speed. What they don't realize is that swinging more slowly is always—and I mean *always*—a rec-ipe for disaster.

To teach Audrey to hit a true second serve, we worked through a series of progressions, in which she learned how to swing in a direction different from the target. This kind of away-from-target swing creates huge amounts of spin. This spin achieves two goals simultaneously: It curves the ball up and over the net, and then it brings it down into the court, making it safe and consistent.

The result is that players like Audrey no longer have to slow down and be careful on second serves. Instead, they can accelerate their rackets confidently while still making a high percentage of serves that are difficult for opponents to handle.

Check out my session with Audrey here:

Case Study 6: The Do-Nothing Volley

Mark is a 4.0 player who drove up from Chicago because he wanted to fix a gaping hole in his game: a complete inability to volley. It's not that Mark refused to approach the net; it's just that anytime he did, it was a total crapshoot, because he couldn't consistently send the ball where he wanted to.

The first thing I noticed when Mark volleyed was that he

had no "feel" or touch. "Feel" sounds like one of those magical tennis talents that you're either gifted with at birth or not, but it's actually nothing like that. "Feel" just means an ability to absorb the power of the incoming ball, instead of inducing power on it. It's a skill that can be learned with practice.

Whenever I teach net play, I begin with what I call the Do-Nothing Volley Drill. Using this and other step-by-step progressions, Mark and I were able to strip away all of his tension, tightness, and overhitting, so he could finally feel the ball on the strings. Once he could do this, Mark could then begin directing the ball to specific spots on the court. Slowly but surely, we built his volley technique from the ground up as Mark learned to apply spin and create depth, making his volley a competitive shot, while maintaining precision and accuracy.

See my work with Mark here:

GLOSSARY OF TENNIS TERMS

Ace A serve that lands in the correct service box but can't be touched by the returning player.

Ad scoring When any game reaches deuce (3 points each player, and every tied score after that), the game can only be won by being ahead 2 points.

Ad side Short for "advantage" side. The left side of the player's side of the court when he or she faces the net.

Alleys Also called "tram lines," they're the long, thin stretch of space on both sides of the court, used only in doubles play (two players per side).

ATP The Association of Tennis Professionals is the governing body of the men's professional tennis circuits—the ATP Tour, the ATP Challenger Tour, and the ATP Champions Tour.

Body serve A serve that travels directly at the body of the returner, making it difficult for him to move out of the way and hit an effective shot.

Break When the player who's serving loses the game.

Contact point Where in relationship to the body the racket is positioned as the ball meets the strings.

Crosscourt Any shot that travels from one side of the court across the center line to the other side of the court, on a diagonal.

Defensive phase of play When a player is off balance, out of position, or otherwise in trouble, giving her opponent the advantage.

Deuce In tennis scoring, when both players reach a score of 40 in a game, or 3 points each. Also, when players are trying to win a game by 2 points, it's what the score is called when they're back to even.

Deuce side The right side of the player's side of the court when he or she is facing the net—called such because it's the side you serve from when the score is deuce.

Down-the-line Any shot that travels straight, staying on the same side of the court it started on (width-wise).

Drop shot A shot purposely hit as short as possible, and often with backspin, into the opponent's court, to force the opponent to run forward to retrieve it.

Error Any shot where a player successfully touches the ball, but it does not land in play on the other side of the court.

Feed The delivery of a tennis ball to a player for the purposes of practice or training. Feeds can be done by yourself, by a coach or training partner, by hand, or with a racket. They can also be done with a ball machine.

Flat serve A serve delivery focused on creating as much speed on the ball as possible, with little to no spin added.

Grand Slams Also called "majors," they're the four most important annual pro tennis events. They offer the most ranking points, prize money, and public and media attention, plus the greatest strength and size of field. They include the US Open, French Open (also called "Roland-Garros"), Australian Open, and Wimbledon.

Ground stroke A shot hit after the ball has bounced on your side of the court. It includes forehands and backhands, whether with topspin, slice, or hit flat ("drives").

Half volley A shot in which the ball is struck extremely low, just above the court surface, immediately after the bounce.

High-percentage tennis Intentionally making safe, high-margin shots to give oneself the best chance of avoiding errors, based on height of the ball over the net, speed, spin, and amount of available court to hit into. High-percentage tennis is not necessarily wimpy or unaggressive; professional players often utilize elements of it until they sense a clear opportunity to attack. It's also important to realize that "safe" is a very relative term. For example, Roger Federer's average forehand speed is 76 miles per hour. That's a routine, controllable speed for elite players, but most amateurs would be hard-pressed to return it with any reliability.

Hold serve When the player who's serving wins the game.

Inside out Receiving a tennis shot angling in toward your body and then sending it back in the direction it came from.

Kick serve A serve hit with a combination of topspin and side-spin that causes the ball to jump higher than a normal bounce, as well as out to the right for a righty and out to the left for a lefty.

Lob A high, arching shot, typically hit very deep. Lobs are designed to sail over an opposing player who's positioned at the net, give a player more time to recover from a poor position, or push opponents deep into their side of the court.

Mini tennis Slow, soft shots hit within the service boxes. Usually used as a warm-up or control drill where both players are rallying back and forth from just behind the service line.

Neutral phase of play When neither player has a clear advantage in a point and the players have equal opportunity to win.

No-ad scoring When any game reaches a deuce point (3 points per player), the game is won by whomever wins the next point—"sudden death."

No-man's-land The wide rectangle positioned across the full width of the back of the singles court. Named such because traditionally players are told to avoid standing in this area of the court, in order to avoid having the ball bounce right at their feet.

NTRP Short for "National Tennis Rating Program," NTRP is a numerical rating system from 1.0 to 7.0, designed to help players identify what level of competition they should play.

Around 90 percent of all tennis players globally play at the 4.0 level or below.

Offensive phase of play When a player is in control and in good balance, and has the opportunity to hit the ball wherever and however she wants.

On the rise Hitting the ball after it bounces but before it reaches the peak of its bounce.

Overhead A shot hit either out of the air or after the bounce from a high, fully extended contact position with an overhand motion.

Passing shot When one opponent is close to the net and the other hits a shot past him from the opposite baseline.

Poach In doubles, to leave the side of the court you started the point on, in order to cut across and intercept the ball before it travels to your partner.

Pusher A playing style that utilizes predominantly safe, non-aggressive shots, in an attempt to outlast one's opponent with consistency alone. Pushers generally don't have any offensive weapons or attacking shots; their only goal is to get the ball back.

Rally When opponents or practice partners hit the ball back and forth.

Risk Purposefully hitting shots with little space over the top of the net and/or close to the lines.

Safety Purposefully hitting shots with plenty of space between the lines and over the net to build in margin for error and avoid errors.

Shadow swing Rehearsing tennis-swing technique without actually hitting a ball.

Shape Curving a tennis shot using spin. Sidespin can curve a shot to the right or left, while topspin curves a shot down toward the court surface.

Slice A ground stroke hit with backspin, where the top of the ball is turning away from the side of the court it's traveling toward; or a serve hit with sidespin where the ball is rotating counterclockwise when hit by a righty, and clockwise when hit by a lefty. A slice in ground strokes is used to change the tempo of a rally and throw off an opponent's timing, as well as to increase the amount of time between shots. A slice in serves is used to curve the shot, making it more likely to land in and challenge an opponent.

Split-step A footwork move that looks like a wide-stanced hop, designed to put the body in an athletic position just as the ball is hit by the opposing player.

Topspin Rotation of the ball where the top is turning forward, toward the direction it's traveling. Topspin is used to curve a tennis shot downward, toward the court surface, allowing a player to aim higher over the net without hitting the ball out.

Unforced error A shot that was missed when a player was well enough positioned, prepared, and balanced to be reasonably expected to make the shot.

Unit turn Preparation of the torso, arms, hands, and racket together into a strong position by coiling the upper body, making smooth, effortless power possible on ground strokes and volleys.

UTR Short for "Universal Tennis Rating," it's a numerical rating from 1.0 to 16.5 designed to help players identify what level of competition they should play.

Volley Any tennis shot hit out of the air, before the ball bounces. Typically shoulder height or below.

Weight transfer The shifting of the body's momentum forward into the ball as contact is made.

Wide serve A serve that bounces close to the outer edge of the service box and travels at an angle off the court, forcing the returner to chase it.

Winner A good shot that lands inside the court and bounces twice, or bounces once and hits a permanent fixture of the court (the fence, umpire chair, etc.), before it can be touched by the opposing player.

WTA The Women's Tennis Association is the principal organizing body of women's professional tennis. It governs the WTA Tour, which is the worldwide professional tennis tour for women and was founded to create a better future for women's tennis.

30 PROGRESSIONS FOR TENNIS IMPROVEMENT

To improve tennis technique, you need to overwrite whatever habits you currently have. The only way to do this is through progressions—step-by-step drills that help you bridge the gap between old, subconscious movement patterns and the new skills you want to master.

Players are often tempted to jump right into the deep end of the pool and immediately use their new forehand, backhand, or serve before actually committing it to muscle memory. They erroneously believe that because they understand *what* they're supposed to do, they can now go out and execute it on court. But the reality is, when players are pressured by the speed and location of a real incoming shot or feel the pressure and anxiety of a real match, they revert to whatever movement patterns they're most familiar with—their old habits.

That's why progressions are vital: Instead of jumping from understanding a new skill to using it in a match, you take a series of small steps toward mastery, one at a time.

Below is a list of thirty progressions you can use for any stroke, footwork pattern, or sequence of targets. I've placed them in order, from easiest to execute to most difficult. The idea is that you build up slowly and steadily, with no sudden jumps—every step is a natural outgrowth of the previous one.

I always recommend beginning with slow shadow swings whenever you first learn a new stroke or technique. Shadow swings allow you to feel the new movements without the pressure of having to hit a ball. I also strongly suggest that at every step, you check yourself on video before moving on to the next, more challenging progression.

Some of these progressions require a hitting partner or coach, but you can also use a ball machine. When you're using a ball machine to work on technique changes for purposeful repetitions, it's crucial that you control the level of challenge. Adjust the settings so the speed of the feed is as slow as possible, while the ball is still being placed in your strike zone. Contact height should be as easy and comfortable as possible. It's equally important to give yourself enough time between shots to process what happened, give yourself reminders, and rehearse a shadow swing before the next ball is fed.

Please note that you likely won't require all thirty progressions to master a new tennis habit. So jump forward to a more difficult progression, and then move back to easier ones as needed, according to the following guidelines:

- If you're unable to perform the new skill perfectly, or close to it, on at least 50 percent of your repetitions, move back to an easier drill progression. Dropping below 50 percent quality repetitions means you're reinforcing your old habit more frequently than training the new one—a recipe for staying stuck!
- If you're able to perform the new skill perfectly or near-perfectly on between 50 and 75 percent of your repetitions, continue training using the same drill progression.
- If you're able to perform the new skill perfectly or close to it on 80 percent or more of your repetitions, move on to a harder drill progression.

When it comes to determining your rate of success, do *not* merely guess based on what you feel or what happens to the ball. Instead, verify the quality of your movements using video—especially before advancing to more challenging training.

The key is to challenge yourself just the right amount: enough so that you don't get bored or feel like you're not progressing, but not so much that you revert back to old habits.

I demonstrate all thirty progressions at www.essential tennis.com/progressions.

PROGRESSIONS

1. Segmented Shadow Swings

   No ball. Slow, smooth movements while making a pause at two or three critical "checkpoints" for the new swing you're trying to master.

2. Continuous Shadow Swings

   No ball. Slow, smooth movements using a steady, continuous tempo throughout the full range of motion.

3. Shadow Swings with Contact "Taps"

   No ball. Smooth, continuous movements where the racket strings are tapping against a fixed object like the net or a wall, to simulate contact with a ball.

4. Fake Tosses

   A ball is tossed but not hit. Instead, use the ball to practice timing the new swing while executing it correctly.

5. Stationary Drop Hits

   Drop a ball to yourself to hit, but without having to move. Hit off one bounce for ground stroke training or in the air for volley training.

6. Drop Hits with Movement
   Drop a ball to yourself to hit, but this time, a bit left,
   right, forward, or backward to induce movement.

7. Close Underhand Toss, same side
   Partner or coach feeds you a ball, underhand, from
   the same side of the net.

8. Far Underhand Toss, other side
   Partner or coach feeds you underhand from the
   other side of the net.

9. Feeds (with racket) from Net (other side), Student
   on Service Line

10. Feeds from Net, Student in No-Man's-Land

11. Feeds from Net, Student on Baseline

12. Feeds from Net, Student on Baseline, with Move-
    ment

13. Feeds from Opposite Service Line

14. Feeds from Opposite No-Man's-Land

15. Feeds from Opposite Baseline

16. Cooperative Rally–Isolated Shot, no target
    "Isolated" means that no other shots are being hit—
    for example, forehand ground strokes being trained
    in isolation without running for backhands, hitting
    serves, or approaching the net. It involves focused,
    repetitive training on one shot in one environment,
    as opposed to integrating it into the larger context of
    playing a full point.

17. Cooperative Rally–Isolated Shot, target area
    "Target area" denotes a large target, like no-man's-

land, one of the service boxes, or half of the court.

18. Cooperative Rally–Isolated Shot, specific target
19. Cooperative Rally–Movement, no target
20. Cooperative Rally–Movement, target area
21. Cooperative Rally–Movement, specific target
22. Cooperative Rally–Starting, with serve

If, for example, you're working on your backhand, you can do so within the context of match play by first hitting a serve or return-of-serve. Complete a serve and *then* hit a backhand, or complete a return-of-serve before you hit a backhand. The return-of-serve itself may also be a backhand, but it's a very different context than within a rally.

23. Cooperative Rally–Starting, with return
24. Competitive Rally–Isolated Shot, specific direction
25. Competitive Rally–Isolated Shot, open direction
26. Competitive Rally–Movement, specific target
27. Competitive Rally–Movement, open direction
28. Competitive Rally–Starting, with serve
29. Competitive Rally–Starting, with return
30. Open Point Play–Sparring

MATCH-SUCCESS CHECKLIST

The Day Before

- **Hydration.** Start fully hydrating your body twelve to twenty-four hours before your scheduled match time. Just plain water is best!
- **Sleep.** Get a solid night's sleep. Aim to be in bed one hour earlier than usual.

Day Of

- **Morning routine.** The morning of your match, eat the breakfast that makes you feel best, drink lots of water, and move through your favorite stretching routine.

- **Lunch.** If your match isn't in the morning, then eat a medium-sized meal an hour and a half to two hours before your scheduled match time. Choose whatever foods make you feel energetic and healthy.
- **Bag check.** An hour before leaving for the court, go through your tennis bag and make sure you have everything you need to play a long match: at least two rackets; extra socks, shirts, shoes, and grips; a water bottle; a towel; fruit and/or energy bars; headphones; Band-Aids and athletic tape; a notebook and pen to write out your Plan A Strategy and make notes on your opponent and the match; and anything else you like having with you on court.
- **Mindset.** Queue up whatever audio gets you in the best mindset for a competitive battle. For some, it's calm, soothing music. For others, it's Metallica. Others still may prefer a podcast or audiobook. Experiment! Get to know yourself and what level of excitement works best for you pre-match.
- **Arrival.** Get to your match venue at least thirty minutes before start time, so you have time to warm up and relax. If there's an open court, hit a few serves and drop-feed a few forehands and backhands to loosen up. If you're a "slow starter," give yourself more time!
- **Twenty minutes before.** Move through a full-body dynamic warm-up, making sure to move smoothly and calmly. Get your heart rate close to playing level in the last five minutes.

- **Pre-match warm-up (part one).** During your hit-around with your opponent, put 80 percent of your attention into evaluating his or her strokes, movement, preferences, strengths, and weaknesses. Which shots do they avoid hitting? Which do they go out of their way to hit? Are they good/bad at the net? How's their serve/return? How much risk do you need to take on to beat this opponent? Use what you learn to construct a game plan.

  Pre-match warm-up (part two). Spend the remaining 20 percent of your warm-up attention on self-evaluation. How's your energy? How do your muscles and joints feel? How does your timing feel? Will you have your normal tool kit of shots today, or will you need to adjust your approach? If you need to adjust, how?

- **Sixty seconds to go.** After the warm-up, spend your final minute constructing a simple yet specific Plan A Strategy to begin the match. Ideally, this plan will include hitting your strengths as often as possible and making your opponent hit what you've identified as their weaknesses as often as possible.

DURING THE MATCH/BETWEEN SETS

- **Hydration.** Drink plenty of water—stay ahead of hydration! If you feel thirsty, it's too late.
- **Adjustments.** During changeovers, make adjustments

to your Plan A. Which patterns are working, and which are not?

- **Attention.** Maintain the 80/20 attention split: 80 percent of your focus should be on what's working/not working for your opponent, 20 percent on yourself.

- **Managing momentum.** If you're crushing your opponent, don't sit down during the changeover! Drink some water and get into position on the other side. Don't give your opponent a chance to regroup. And vice versa: If you're losing badly, use all the time you legally have to slow things down.

- **Game plan.** Remember: Always change a losing game plan and never change a winning one!

Acknowledgments

Let's face it: Tennis can be a lonely sport. So can entrepreneurship and content creation. That's why I feel so blessed to have had the encouragement and support of so many people over the years. Those people made this book possible.

Thank you, God, for blessing me with the energy, motivation, and passions that I have, and for placing so many incredible people in my path to make my career and this book a reality.

Ted Sprinkmann, my childhood coach, taught me what it means to live what you love. He inspired me to follow in his footsteps and make tennis my career.

My parents, Paul and Linda, gave me the freedom to pursue what I loved and choose my own path.

Alison, my wife of seventeen years, has believed in me from the start. She supported my decision to transition from a nontraditional career path to an even less established one. She nurtures our children and manages our home, so that I have the time and energy to pursue the crazy ideas in my head.

Joel, my cowriter, took my philosophies about tennis, broke them down, and reassembled them into beautifully written words. In doing so, he made my lifelong dream of publishing a book a reality.

Dan Lazar, my literary agent, put the quality and integrity of this book first and served as an inspiring example of how to constantly and continually strive for excellence.

Tim at St. Martin's Press believed strongly in this book from the moment it landed on his desk. His excitement and passion from the perspective of a tennis player pursuing his own breakthroughs made our collaboration all the more fulfilling.

To the coaches who left safety and stability to come alongside me at Essential Tennis: I'm grateful to you for believing in my vision and joining me on the tightrope walk of translating our life's work to the internet. You've all taught me so much. Thank you, Ira, Kirby, Megan, and Kevin.

I've had the privilege to team up with production professionals who've worked tirelessly to make my thoughts and explanations as engaging and interesting as possible. Your creativity and dedication inspires me daily. Thank you, James, Tyler, Gabriel, and Craig.

Thank you, Will Hamilton, for being my friend and mentor. Time and again, you held out a helping hand as I stumbled through the early years of content and course creation.

To the marketing and growth experts who have treated my business as their own and pushed hard to help me reach as many tennis players as possible—thank you, Justin, Jefreaux, Jerhad, and Brian, for helping me make a bigger impact than I otherwise would have.

Dozens of other tennis coaches and players have shared their insights, triumphs, and failures with me and online for the world to see every day. You inspire me to keep learning, to be more vulnerable, and to share more of myself. I respect you all so much: Jeff Salzenstein at Tennis Evolution; Tomaz Mercinger at Feel Tennis; Peter Freeman at Crunch Time Coaching; Brady and Mark at Daily Tennis Lesson; Simon and Alex at Top Tennis Training; Karue Sell at My Tennis HQ; Scott and Nate at Play Your Court; Dayday Kay at Racket Flex; Ashley Neaves at The Tennis Mentor; Brian Dabul; Mehrban Iranshad at Tennis Files; Milan Krnjetin at TenFitMen; Jason at TennisUnleashed; P. J. Simmons at the Tennis Congress; Jorge Capestany at TennisDrills.TV; Florian, Nadim, Gregg, and Ean at Online Tennis Instruction; Tim Moy; Ramon Osa; Mark Sansait; and Craig O'Shannessy, whose insights and statistics were incredibly helpful.

There are countless others doing amazing work for the tennis community online. Thank you all.

And of course, my students: Your passion, effort, and

dedication are what fuel me to keep creating and publishing. Thank you for supporting me with every like, comment, course registration, and clinic sign-up. You have enabled me to pursue what I love, and for that, I'll be eternally grateful.

I. W.

Thank you:

Ian Westermann, for inviting me to collaborate with you on this incredible project. You've taught me so much about tennis. More important, you've allowed me to declare all of my tennis gear as tax-deductible. Let's write another book soon!

Dan Lazar, the absolute best literary agent on planet Earth.

Tim Bartlett, Alice Pfeifer, and the fantastic team at St. Martin's Press. Your suggestions took this book from 4.5 to 7.0. Tennis players know what I mean.

Dorit and the Fantastic Four for, well, everything.

J.C.

ABOUT THE AUTHORS

IAN WESTERMANN is the founder of EssentialTennis.
com, the world's number one online tennis instruction
portal launched in 2011. After graduating college, he
took a job at Congressional Country Club in Bethesda,
Maryland. Now, Westermann and his staff of coaches,
content planners, and production crew guide the improvement of thousands of students from every corner
of the world—more than one hundred forty countries in
all. Westermann lives in Milwaukee with his family.

JOEL CHASNOFF is a stand-up comedian and author
of three books, including the memoir *The 188th Cry-
baby Brigade*. A Chicago native, he currently splits his
time between Austin, Texas, and Tel Aviv. Visit him at
www.joelchasnoff.com.